2004

NEW DIRECTIONS FOR CHILD DEVELOPMENT

William Damon, *Brown University*
EDITOR-IN-CHIEF

Father-Adolescent Relationships

Shmuel Shulman
Bar Ilan University

W. Andrew Collins
University of Minnesota

EDITORS

Number 62, Winter 1993

JOSSEY-BASS PUBLISHERS
San Francisco

FATHER-ADOLESCENT RELATIONSHIPS
Shmuel Shulman, W. Andrew Collins (eds.)
New Directions for Child Development, no. 62
William Damon, Editor-in-Chief

Microfilm copies of issues and articles are available in 16mm and 35mm, as well as microfiche in 105mm, through University Microfilms Inc., 300 North Zeeb Road, Ann Arbor, Michigan 48106-1346.

LC 85-644581   ISSN 0195-2269   ISBN 0-7879-9959-8

NEW DIRECTIONS FOR CHILD DEVELOPMENT is part of The Jossey-Bass Education Series and is published quarterly by Jossey-Bass Inc., Publishers, 350 Sansome Street, San Francisco, California 94104-1342 (publication number USPS 494-090). Second-class postage paid at San Francisco, California, and at additional mailing offices. POSTMASTER: Send address changes to Jossey-Bass Inc., Publishers, 350 Sansome Street, San Francisco, California 94104-1342.

EDITORIAL CORRESPONDENCE should be sent to the Editor-in-Chief, William Damon, Department of Education, Box 1938, Brown University, Providence, Rhode Island 02912.

Cover photograph by Wernher Krutein/PHOTOVAULT © 1990.

Manufactured in the United States of America. Nearly all Jossey-Bass books, jackets, and periodicals are printed on recycled paper that contains at least 50 percent recycled waste, including 10 percent postconsumer waste. Many of our materials are also printed with vegetable-based inks; during the printing process, these inks emit fewer volatile organic compounds (VOCs) than petroleum-based inks. VOCs contribute to the formation of smog.

CONTENTS

W. Andrew Collins
Recent research has moved beyond documenting links between father behavior and adolescent behavior to address possible processes governing relationships with adolescents, including contextual factors associated with variations in relationships.

EDITORS' NOTES

Two decades ago Lamb (1975, p. 246) described fathers as "forgotten contributors to child development." Since that time, investigations into fathers' interactions with their children and their impact on development have followed a rapidly rising trajectory (Collins and Russell, 1991; Lamb and Oppenheim, 1989). Most of these studies have focused on the extent of paternal involvement with offspring and comparisons of behavioral roles of fathers and mothers (Lamb, Pleck, Charnov, and Levine, 1987; Russell and Russell, 1987). Findings have consistently showed that fathers, compared with mothers, spend less time with their children across all ages (Berman and Pederson, 1987; Lamb, 1987; Montemayor and Brownlee, 1987; Russell, 1983). Fathers also have been found to be less engaged and to take less responsibility in caregiving activities, although they are reported to be more involved in physical and outdoor play activities. Although most of these studies involved early and middle childhood samples, the studies of adolescents also revealed the lower involvement of fathers and the prevalence of leisure or play in their shared activities (Montemayor and Brownlee, 1987; Russell, 1983).

Fathers' relatively low engagement with their young children may be attributable to persisting gender differences in the amount of time devoted to out-of-home work roles. This is less compelling, however, as an explanation for the differences between father-adolescent and mother-adolescent relationships. Adolescents spend longer periods of time away from parents (Larson and Richards, 1991) and are less dependent on parents' immediate caretaking activities than younger children. Fathers' behavioral roles, then, need not be related to their immediacy and to whether they are drawn (or not drawn) into caregiving. Broader understanding of father and mother roles in child development could be achieved by exploring the role of fathers from historical, sociological, and ethological perspectives.

Models of Fatherhood in Nature and in History

In a recent provocative paper Kraemer (1991) proposed that fatherhood is a human invention. Observations of animals, and especially mammals who resemble humans in the prolonged caregiving of their offspring, indicate that males are not active partners in family life. According to Goodall (1986), male chimpanzees are little involved with the caretaking of the younger generation. Females and children live in separate bands from males. Males are interested in the females only when they are in estrus. Because females may be mated by multiple males, paternity is often in doubt. In other species, males may not be totally separated from their offspring, but involvement is limited. Among wolves, for example, mothers lick, nuzzle, clean the excrement of, and carry the young offspring. Males rarely carry the young and are minimally engaged with them, but they maintain proximity to protect mother and offspring from unexpected predators. Even in the few instances of caregiving by males, the father's role is secondary to that of the mother (Zimen, 1971). This pattern of separate or peripheral father involvement characterizes the large majority of mammalian species.

A similar pattern is found among the Aka pygmies, a hunter-gatherer society (Hewlett, 1987). In Aka society, the father's position in relation to the offspring is peripheral. Kraemer (1991) argues that the shift from hunter-gatherer to agricultural modes and the domestication of animals required a more organized social life. Obtaining sufficient food required more labor in cultivation of crops and in herding of animals. More labor meant that more workers were needed; consequently, women were more in demand for producing babies. Men increasingly perceived not only their agricultural products and livestock, but also their women and offspring, as their property. Kraemer traces the increasing control of men and the emergence of the concept of patriarchy to these early changes.

Social, economic, and religious reformation during the seventeenth century intensified the father's control over his household. Some powers formerly given to religious leaders and royal rulers were transferred to the nuclear family headed by the father. Fathers were expected not only to protect and provide, but also to wield legal, moral, and religious authority. Further significant changes occurred following the industrial revolution in the mid-nineteenth century (Hareven, 1982). Families left the farms, and men became factory workers. Factory work often required more than ten hours per day, six days per week, leaving little time for men to spend with their families. Though men became the primary wage earners, the woman's role as sole guardian and nurturer of children increased. Men returning home tired from work were not expected to take care of their children. Fathers again became peripheral figures in their families. Mackey (1985) described men's role in society during this period as protector/solicitor and provider and women's role as primary caregiver. This distinction between male and female roles, combined with the supremacy of men, is similar to the gender distinction in hunter-gatherer and agricultural times.

Parsons and Bales (1956) described the father as the instrumental leader of the family, whose role is to be the breadwinner and to interact with the external world, and the mother as the expressive leader of the family, whose role is to provide emotional support for family members and to contribute to well-being within the family. During the past two decades the growing number of women in the workforce—many of whom contribute significantly, even equally, to family income—has intensified questions about the role of fathers. What former models and current needs should guide the redefiniton of fathers' role? Contributions to this volume deal with these questions and, more specifically, with the role of fathers during the adolescent years of their offspring.

Fathers of Adolescents: Possible Models

Analysis of fatherhood in nature and throughout history suggests two basic models. The first, found in many species and through many stages of history, is the father who does not take an active role in the upbringing of his children but assumes the responsibility to protect his family and to provide it with basic needs. This model implies that fathers are distinctive from mothers. Support for this contention can be found in evidence that, even when fathers are highly involved in caretaking, their style of interaction with their children remains distinct from maternal styles (Yogman, 1982). Whereas mothers and infants may be observed to have tender dialogues, fathers and their infants may engage in what Herzog (1982) described as a "kamikaze mode" of play, in which fathers throw the baby into the air like a plaything. These distinctive styles of father-child and mother-child interaction have been attributed to higher levels of aggression among males (Ross, 1985).

An additional contrast between males and females concerns perceptions of close relationships. Whereas males express themselves in terms of separateness and insist on their independence, females perceive themselves as embedded in relationships and regard it important to secure their connectedness (Gilligan, 1982). Females have been found more likely than males to express intimacy and to be open and self-disclosing (Clark and Reis, 1988). It is therefore reasonable to assume that fathers' and mothers' relationships with their children are distinctive.

The second model suggests that fatherhood may be flexible in response to varying circumstances. Under conditions of increased need for caretaking, fathers may become almost primary caregivers. When conditions require the father to become involved—when, for example, he becomes unemployed or has lost his partner—the father is perfectly capable of acquiring the necessary skills (Levine, 1976; Russell, 1983). Lamb claimed that fathers cede responsibility to mothers because of fathers' lesser experience in parenting, but these differences are not irreversible (Lamb and Oppenheim, 1989, p. 14). Nowadays, when both parents commonly work outside the home, fathers may be more similar to mothers in their behavior and attitudes toward their children.

Adolescence is a transitory period during which the individual moves from childhood to adulthood. The basic task during adolescence is to attain the ability to manage separation from parents, both in physical distance and in the psychological and emotional capacity for sustained separateness (Constantine, 1987). Adolescents are supposed to renegotiate relationships with parents. What role do parents, specifically fathers, employ in this renegotiation process? Do fathers stick to their traditional, less engaged role, as conceptualized in the first model of fatherhood? If so, what is the implication of such a model of fatherhood for the nature of fathers' interactions with their adolescents? Or do fathers who tend to become more involved with their children, as implied by the second model of fatherhood, have some difficulties with their offspring's striving for autonomy as mothers do? Two contributions to this volume represent studies reflecting the two respective models. Shmuel Shulman and Moshe Klein explore the possible distinctive contribution of fathers to adolescent development and individuation. Reed W. Larson's paper, more representative of the model that describes that changing role of fatherhood, covers the dilemmas fathers have once their children reach adolescence.

The preceding questions suggest that fathers of adolescents may face two dilemmas: what model of fatherhood to adopt and what role of fatherhood is more suitable with adolescent offspring. It is mainly in Western cultures that men and women are expected to adapt to changes in gender roles and in models of parenting (Pleck, 1981) and therefore face uncertainties regarding the appropriate attitude to take toward their adolescents. Other cultures have norms and scripts regarding the individuation process of their adolescents. In Papua New Guinea adolescent boys are separated from their mothers in order to sever the symbiotic bond between the mother and the adolescent; males take an active role in transforming the adolescent boy into an adult member of the society (Bosse, 1990). In Mexican-American subcultures, fathers may be very affectionate with their young children and even be an active caregiver if the mother is the primary breadwinner (Madsen, 1973). Yet when children enter puberty, fathers' attitudes become more authoritarian (Mirande, 1988). Fathers may even use excessive violence to discipline adolescents and enforce family norms. The contribution by Catherine Cooper, Harley Baker, Dina Polichar, and Mara Welsh presents variations in adolescents' perceptions of the balance between separateness and connectedness in various ethnic groups. Of special interest is the mediating role of values of familism in non–European American cultures.

So far the emphasis has been on different models of fatherhood and the implications of various models for adolescent development. Development does not end, however, in adolescence. For example, the midlife stage of parents' development often corresponds to adolescence in their children. According to Combrinck-Graham (1985), midlife issues can be perceived from a family perspective. Family life oscillates between two tendencies. The first emphasizes closeness and cohesion among family members and is strongly evident during infancy. As children grow older, they tend to distance themselves from the family. It is not only children, however, who strive for independence. Parents as well may wish for more space of their own and therefore encourage youngsters' movement toward greater autonomy. Career issues are also common during this period. Stress associated with midlife issues may affect fathers' relationships with their adolescents, as documented in the chapter by Raymond Montemayor, Patrick C. McKenry, and Teresa Julian.

This volume grew out of the symposium Father-Adolescent Relationships: Perspectives on Their Nature and Developmental Significance, presented at the 1992 biennial meeting of the Society for Research on Adolescence in Washington, D.C. David Almeida and Nancy Galambos graciously agreed to join the participants of that symposium by contributing to this volume.

We express our appreciation to each of the authors. All were unfailingly cooperative, some despite personal adversity and severe time pressures. We also are grateful to Lonnie Behrendt, who played an invaluable role in coordinating communications among multiple authors and editors on four different contents.

Shmuel Shulman
W. Andrew Collins
Editors

References

Berman, P. W., and Pederson, F. A. "Research on Men's Transitions to Parenthood: An Integrative Discussion." In P. W. Berman and F. A. Pedersen (eds.), *Men's Transitions to Parenthood: Longitudinal Studies of Early Family Experience.* Hillsdale, N.J.: Erlbaum, 1987.

Bosse, H. "Violence and Care: The Appropriation of 'Sons' by Their 'Fathers' in Papua New Guinea." *Group Analysis,* 1990, *23,* 5–16.

Clark, M. S., and Reis, H. T. "Interpersonal Processes in Close Relationships." *Annual Review of Psychology,* 1988, *39,* 609–672.

Collins, W. A., and Russell, G. "Mother-Child and Father-Child Relationships in Middle Childhood and Adolescence: A Developmental Analysis." *Developmental Review,* 1991, *11,* 99–136.

Combrinck-Graham, L. "A Developmental Model for Family Systems." *Family Process,* 1985, *24,* 139–150.

Constantine, L. L. "Adolescent Processes and Family Organization: A Model of Development as a Function of Family Paradigm." *Journal of Adolescent Research,* 1987, *2,* 349–366.

Gilligan, C. *In a Different Voice.* Cambridge, Mass.: Harvard University Press, 1982.

Goodall, J. *The Chimpanzees of Gombe Patterns of Behavior.* Cambridge, Mass.: Belknap Press, 1986.

Hareven, T. *Family Time and Industrial Time.* New York: Cambridge University Press, 1982.

Herzog, J. "Patterns of Expectant Fatherhood." In S. Cath (ed.), *Father and Child.* Boston: Little, Brown, 1982.

Hewlett, B. "Intimate Fathers: Patterns of Paternal Holding Among Aka Pygmies." In M. E. Lamb (ed.), *The Father's Role: Cross Cultural Perspectives.* Hillsdale, N.J.: Erlbaum, 1987.

Kraemer, S. "The Origins of Fatherhood: An Ancient Family Process." *Family Process,* 1991, *30,* 377–392.

Lamb, M. E. "Fathers: Forgotten Contributors to Child Development." *Human Development,* 1975, *18,* 245–266.

Lamb, M. E. *The Father's Role: Cross Cultural Perspectives.* Hillsdale, N.J.: Erlbaum, 1987.

Lamb, M. E., and Oppenheim, D. "Fatherhood and Father-Child Relationships: Five Years of Research." In S. H. Cath, A. Gurwitt, and L. Gunsberg (eds.), *Fathers and Their Families.* Hillsdale, N.J.: Analytic Press, 1989.

Lamb, M. E., Pleck, J. H., Charnov, E. L., and Levine, J. A. "A Biosocial on Paternal Behavior and Involvement." In J. B. Lancaster, J. Altman, A. Rossi, and L. R. Sherrod (eds.), *Parenting Across the Life Span.* Chicago: Aldine, 1987.

Larson, R. W., and Richards, M. H. "Daily Companionship in Late Childhood and Early Adolescence: Changing Developmental Contexts." *Child Development,* 1991, *62,* 284–300.

Levine, J. A. *And Who Will Raise the Children.* Philadelphia: Lippincott, 1976.

MacKey, W. C. "A Cross-Cultural Perspective on Perceptions of Paternalistic Deficiencies in the US: The Myth of the Derelict Daddy." *Sex Roles,* 1985, *12,* 509–533.

Madsen, M. *The Mexican-American of South Texas.* New York: Holt, Rinehart & Winston, 1973.

Mirande, A. "Chicano Fathers." In P. Bornstein and C. P. Cowan (eds.), *Fatherhood Today: Men's Changing Role in the Family.* New York: Wiley, 1988.

Montemayor, R., and Brownlee, J. R. "Fathers, Mothers and Adolescents: Gender Based Differences in Parental Roles During Adolescence." Journal of Youth and Adolescence, 1987, 16, 281–291.

Parsons, T. E., and Bales, J. R. Family, Socialization, and Interaction Process. New York: Free Press, 1955.

Pleck, J. H. The Myth of Masculinity. Cambridge, Mass.: MIT Press, 1981.

Ross, J. H. "The Darker Side of Fatherhood: Clinical and Developmental Ramifications of the 'Lewis Motif.'" Psychoanalytic Study of the Child, 1985, 40, 117–144.

Russell, G. The Changing Role of Fathers. Brisbane, Australia: University of Queensland Press, 1983.

Russell, G., and Russell, A. "Mother-Child and Father-Child Relationships in Middle Childhood." Child Development, 1987, 58, 1573–1585.

Yogman, M. "The Effects of the Father-Infant Relationship." In S. Cath (ed.), Father and Child. Boston: Little, Brown, 1982.

Ziemen, E. Woffe und Konigspudel, Verglichende Verhaltensbeobachtuegen. Munich, Germany: Piper, 1971.

SHMUEL SHULMAN is in the Department of Psychology at Bar Ilan University, Ramat Gan, Israel. His main interests are adolescent development and family systems and therapy.

W. ANDREW COLLINS is professor in the Institute of Child Development, University of Minnesota.

Difficulties in relationships between young adolescents and their fathers arise from the daily conditions under which their lives intersect.

Finding Time for Fatherhood: The Emotional Ecology of Adolescent-Father Interactions

Reed W. Larson

"When I'm upset," said John Niles, an emotive forty-two-year-old sales manager and father of two, "I project it out, I react negatively to people; and often I close in and withdraw." Marital research shows that men frequently exhibit these two reactions, anger and withdrawal, in conflicts with their wives (Gottman, 1991; Gottman and Levenson, 1986). John described them as common responses in his interactions with his elder, thirteen-year-old son, Luke. John related how, after coming home from his job, he used to easily "fly off the handle." As a young adolescent, Luke was trying out new behaviors and testing his autonomy; for John there would always be something in Luke's behavior to get him upset. Sometimes John expressed his·anger directly at Luke; sometimes he turned on the TV and disengaged. The result, in both cases, was a feeling of alienation between father and son.

Research with European-American samples has found this kind of alienation to be common between fathers and their adolescent children. Teenagers in this cultural group experience their fathers as more authoritarian, more distant, and less sensitive to significant personal issues in their lives compared with their mothers (Collins and Russell, 1991; Youniss and Smollar, 1985). Adolescents are going through major life changes, and many perceive their fathers to be out of touch with these changes. What research has yet to

This research was supported by National Institute of Mental Health grant number MH38324, awarded to Reed Larson; grant number MH42618, awarded to Maryse H. Richards; and a National Research Service Award to Reed Larson.

elucidate is how this alienation is related to the types of daily scenarios John described and the factors that lie behind these scenarios.

Family relations need to be understood in the context of family members' hour-to-hour lives. In John's case, his work situation was an important factor in shaping his interactions with his adolescent son. Since John's wife was not employed, he bore the full brunt of breadwinning for the family. During the period he was describing, John held an extremely high-pressure job. The result was that he would arrive home exhausted, with little reserve of energy and a low frustration tolerance. He would also bring home a feeling that he had done battle for the family; he was now entitled to take care of his own needs and not have to put up with anyone else's. John's responses of projection and withdrawal, then, were related to his exertion at work and the privileges that he felt followed from that exertion.

In this chapter I first examine the historical background of the father's daily role within the European-American, two-parent family. Although John's situation of being the sole breadwinner is becoming less common, the legacy of this traditional role still structures men's interactions with their families, including their adolescent children. In the bulk of the chapter I present research on how relationships between fathers and adolescents are enacted in daily life: How often and when do they interact? What emotional state does each bring to the interactions? How do the father's and adolescent's daily realities set up or handicap their relationship? I focus on relationships of fathers with adolescents in the ten-to-fourteen age period because this is a time of major change in young people's lives, when they often report diminished understanding from their fathers (Youniss and Ketterlinus, 1987). The issue is, what can we learn about the typical daily scenarios of father-adolescent interactions that might help us make this relationship more vital?

Divergent Realities of Fathers and Adolescents

Legacy of Men's Breadwinner Role. Fathers' lives take their shape, in part, from the historical evolution of the father and husband role. As families left the farm in the nineteenth and early twentieth centuries, fathers became the primary wage earner, in many cases working six-day, sixty-hour-per-week jobs. The burden of ensuring their families' economic well-being took up most of their time, and what little they had left over was spent recuperating from these demands. This meant they often had little time and energy for involvement in the daily lives of their families. Women provided a greater financial contribution to families than is commonly believed (Hareven, 1982); nonetheless, men were seen as bearing the responsibility for the family's financial needs (Bernard, 1981; Hood, 1986).

For many men the job also became an end in itself. Being a skilled butcher, an effective foreman, or a reputable doctor was the central medium through which a man developed his identity as an adult. And the peak of his career usually corresponded (and still does) with the age at which his children reached adolescence.

This concentration of men's energies on their jobs was reinforced by the parallel evolution of the woman's family role. During the same period that men became breadwinners, a new ideology promoted the woman's role as guardian of the home sphere and nurturer of children. Mothers came to be viewed as "professional homemakers," and this further excluded men from the daily lives of their families (Pleck, 1976). Child-care books at the turn of the century rarely mentioned fathers; and as recently as the 1950s such books declared that the father's foremost task was to provide for the family, and his secondary responsibility was not direct care to his children, but providing emotional support to his wife (Goodman, 1959). In effect, a man's relationship to his children was depersonalized: he was valued not for his personal qualities but for the money he brought in. Fatherhood was a "Sunday Institution"; father was often either a "guest or a ghost" in the home (Katz, 1953); and father's ignorance and ineptitude with household matters were often a matter of public humor (Demos, 1982).

The few direct responsibilities that fathers had toward their adolescent children—discipline, and being an ambassador to the outside world (Gecas, 1976; Johannis, 1957)—were hardly ones that made for close relationships. Descriptions of fatherhood from as recently as thirty-five years ago now strike us as bizarre, such as the following quote from a reputable parent advice book published in 1959: "A boy needs a man in his life to show him how to fight hard, play fair and swear properly—how to be a man! A girl needs a father, too, to be her first beau, to bring out those feminine graces in her with which she will later capture a good husband" (Goodman, 1959, p. 123). With such injunctions being given to fathers in the not-too-distant past, it is no wonder that many have difficulty establishing close relations with their adolescent children.

Fathers' Daily Lives. The lives of most adult men are still strongly influenced by this traditional definition of their role. They grew up witnessing their own fathers enact this role, and most have not had the opportunity to learn anything different. Even though the amount of time fathers put into their jobs has steadily declined since the turn of the century (Pleck, 1986; Stafford and Duncan, 1985), and even though women's labor force participation has dramatically increased in recent decades, the legacy of the old role structure is alive and well. Survey research finds that a majority of fathers *and mothers* still identify the breadwinner role as men's primary responsibility to the family (Hood, 1986; Lein, 1979; Pleck, 1985). In two-parent families the father's wage is still usually seen as primary and the wage of a working mother is often seen as supplementary (Perry-Jenkins and Crouter, 1990). Furthermore, men's identities are still strongly anchored in their jobs (Levinson, 1978), as is particularly evident in their sense of decimation when they are unemployed (Jahoda, 1982).

The continuing influence of men's traditional breadwinner role is evident in the emotional pattern of fathers' daily lives. When interrupted at random times during their jobs, the fathers in our study reported working hard. Compared with employed mothers, they reported higher rates of absorption at work, greater competitiveness, and more frequent situations in which they were cast as the leader. Associated with this, they reported feeling less happiness at work than at home and than employed women at their jobs. They reported more frequent feelings of frustration, irritability, and nervousness (Larson and Richards, in press). Within the structure of their day, work was where these men invested their strain.

The traditional corollary of men's exertion at their jobs is their claim to spending home time as they please. We found that men exercise the discretion to spend a majority of their nonwork time in leisure and personal-care activities, and they do this whether or not the wife is employed. They also report more choice over what they do in the home sphere: even when they do family work, they see it as more voluntary (Larson and Richards, in press). Men feel that their role as primary breadwinner justifies their carrying little responsibility for family work (Perry-Jenkins and Crouter, 1990). Because they have worked hard all day and "sacrificed" for their families, fathers claim a sense of entitlement, whether justified or not, to relax and do what they want when they come home.

We also found that, after difficult days at work, men often bring negative emotions home, and these get transmitted to their wives and adolescent children. This emotional "carryover" and "crossover" has also been detected by other researchers (Crouter, Perry-Jenkins, Huston, and Crawford, 1989; Repetti, 1989).

Men's participation as fathers of adolescents, then, occurs within this context. It is structured by men's jobs, by the emotions they bring home from these jobs, and by their interpretation of the privileges these jobs grant them. Survey data show that men place extreme importance on their families: they want to be involved; they want to be nurturant and concerned fathers (Pleck, 1985). But they also come home from work with a sense of entitlement to leisure that conditions their relationships to their adolescent children.

Adolescents' Daily Lives. Adolescents live in a reality that is markedly different from that of their fathers, and the divergence between these realities sets the stage for their daily interactions.

Young adolescents are in the midst of a set of major life changes that affect all aspects of their experience. These include puberty, cognitive changes, and often the change to junior high or middle school. They are also subject to an increased likelihood of idiosyncratic stressful events, such as those associated with dating (Larson and Ham, 1993). The result of these changes is that they experience more frequent negative emotion during their daily lives than do preadolescents. Events at school, conflicts with friends, and disappointments in romance trigger more occasions of anger, worry, and unhappiness (Larson and Asmussen, 1991; Larson and Ham, 1993). Compared with their fathers, adolescents report more times when they feel unhappy, angry, nervous, embarrassed, and self-conscious (Larson and Richards, in press).

During this same developmental period, the position of family experience within adolescents' daily reality is changing. Like their dads, young adolescents spend about half of their waking hours at home and half away from home, but the meaning and emotional experience of this time is different for adolescents, and it is changing. Young adolescents report increasing behavioral and emotional autonomy from their families (Steinberg and Silverberg, 1986). The amount of time they spend with their families falls dramatically, as they spend more time alone in their rooms. In addition, the emotional states young adolescents report when with family become less consistently positive (Larson and Richards, 1991). Life away from home, particularly with friends, becomes more enthralling.

Family remains an important emotional base: adolescents feel calmer and less self-conscious in the presence of their families than elsewhere (Larson, 1988), and they report valuing their parents (Youniss and Smollar, 1985). Yet, at the same time, they often feel unsatisfied with their relationships to their fathers (Youniss and Smollar, 1985).

Relationships Between Fathers and Adolescents. Research indicates that the same general qualities that make for good mothering make for good fathering. Being responsive, attentive, and warm are criteria of good parenting for both mother and father (Dix, 1991; Lamb, 1987). Adolescents want a close, sensitive relationship with their fathers (Youniss and Smollar, 1985). The question is, do the lives of adolescents and fathers allow them to cultivate these qualities? In a time sampling study, my colleagues and I attempted to obtain direct data on how adolescents' changing reality meshes or clashes with fathers' daily cycles of work and recuperation.

A Study of Family Time and Emotion

My findings come from a study of the daily lives of 55 young adolescents, their mothers, and their fathers, carried out with Maryse H. Richards from Loyola University of Chicago. These family members carried electronic pagers for one week and provided reports on their experience when signaled at random times, following procedures of the Experience Sampling Method (ESM) (Csikszentmihalyi and Larson, 1987). From these reports we are able to describe the daily intersection of fathers' and young adolescents' lives.

The sample of fifty-five families comes from two Chicago suburbs, one working-class and one middle-class, and closely approximates the characteristics of these two communities. Participants were recruited from the families of fifth to eighth graders in four schools. Although not a random sample, the fifty-five families resembled the two-parent families in a larger, more representative sample used in another study (Larson and Richards, 1989). All were two-parent families of European and Eastern European descent. Fathers ranged in age from 29 to 53 (M = 39.3, SD = 5.2). All but one dad had completed high school; 38 percent had completed college. The young adolescents came from fifth- to eighth-grade classrooms and were approximately evenly distributed by grade, sex, and community.

Our objective was to obtain a sample of family members' typical experience. Fathers, mothers, and young adolescents carried pagers during the same week and received signals simultaneously. One signal was sent within each two-hour block between 7:30 A.M. and 9:30 P.M. for seven days. Participants were asked to respond to as many signals as possible and not to share their self-reports with each other. In total, the young adolescents responded to a median of forty-five signals and the fathers to a median of forty-three, representing a response rate of close to 90 percent. Our data thus cover the great majority of their daily lives.

Participants reported their experience at each signal in a booklet containing a set of identical self-report forms. These forms included items asking about their situation and subjective state at the time of each signal. For their situations, I consider here their reports of their companionship and activity. They reported who they were with on a fixed response item, and they reported what they were doing on an open-ended item, for which responses have been coded into mutually exclusive categories with an agreement rate maintained above 94 percent.

My analysis of subjective states focuses on a scale of "affect" that provides an index of whether the emotional state was positive or negative. It was computed from the sum of three 7-point semantic differential items (happy-unhappy, cheerful-irritable, friendly-angry). Prior analyses show that responses on this scale are reliable and demonstrate construct validity (Larson, 1989a, 1989b). For the analyses here, raw affect scores have been converted to z-scores by subtracting each individual's overall mean and dividing by his or her standard deviation. This transformation provides a score that represents a respondent's feelings in a situation relative to the rest of his or her experience. It should be noted that nearly everyone's mean score was above the neutral point on the raw affect scale; thus negative scores on the z-scale do not necessarily correspond to negative affect.

I employ a measure of warmth obtained from the self-report forms. On being signaled, each person rated how "close to," "friendly toward," and "relaxed" he or she felt in relation to the two other family members in the study. These ratings were summed across all beeper sheets to create an index of the level of warmth in the relationship. Scores for this scale have a substantial correlation with the child's rating on a questionnaire measure of "closeness" (Blyth, 1982) (r = .51 for child's warmth toward father; r = .35 for father's warmth toward the child). While the ad hoc nature of this measure should be recognized, substantial correlations with measures of the adolescents' well-being (Larson and Richards, in press) also suggest it may approximate other measures of warmth discussed in the parenting literature.

Finally, several open-ended questions on the ESM form elicited descriptions of the situations people were in and the explanations for their emotional states. I have used responses to these items and data from interviews with the participants to provide examples that illustrate the findings.

Time Fathers and Young Adolescents Share. The first question I wanted to ask was simply, when and how often did these fathers and adolescents interact? In what situations did they report being together? Since participants in the research were paged at random times across their waking hours, the frequency of the situations they reported allows us to estimate how often and under what conditions adolescents and fathers are with each other.

Fathers reported spending a substantial amount of their available time in the vicinity of their adolescent children. They reported being with the child in the study in 27 percent of their reports, which is not that much less than the 36 percent reported by mothers. They do appear to be putting in time with their adolescent children. In fact, fathers reported being in the presence of the target adolescent child for about half of the times that they were not at work or commuting to work. Given that the average father in our sample left for work at 6:45 A.M. and did not get home from work until 5:30 P.M., it is not surprising that approximately half, 47 percent, of this time was on weekends.

Though it appears that fathers were putting in hours with their adolescent children, most of this shared time was not direct interaction, as is evident in Figure 1.1. First, it is striking that, although the two groups were signaled at the same moment, adolescents often did not agree with their fathers on the times when they were together. Sometimes the father said they were together when the teen said they were not, as happened when a father was clearing the table and his daughter was reading a book in the adjoining room. Less often, the teenager said they were together when the father said they were not. This rate of disagreement was comparable with that between mothers and adolescents, indicating that for both parents there are many occasions when being "with" the adolescent is ambiguous.

Second, even for the times when father and teenager agreed they were together, mothers were also present for a majority of these times. Adolescents reported their mothers to be present for 77 percent of these times and fathers for 65 percent. This presence of the mother is important because research by Gjerde (1986) indicates that in these triangular situations, fathers are often marginal participants. They are likely to be passive and disengaged. In one case a girl and her mother were having a bitter argument in the car, and her father, who was driving, appeared to be ignoring both of them. During many of these times when fathers and adolescents were together, the extent of the father's involvement appeared to be minimal.

Thus the amount of time fathers and young adolescents agreed they were together, without the mother present, was quite small. It accounted for 3.6 percent of waking hours (as compared with 8.9 percent between mothers and adolescents, without fathers). And for only one-third of this time did fathers and adolescents report the same activity. We do find that the amount of one-

Figure 1.1. Amount of Time Adolescents and Their Fathers Report Being Together

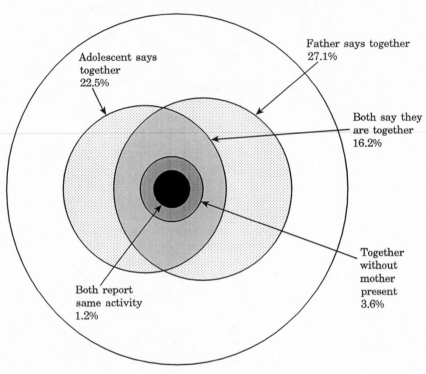

Adolescent says together 22.5%

Father says together 27.1%

Both say they are together 16.2%

Together without mother present 3.6%

Both report same activity 1.2%

Note: Percentages are for waking hours between 7:30 A.M. and 9:30 P.M.

on-one time between adolescents and their fathers is stable with the adolescent's age. Fathers do not become any more disengaged as the adolescent grows older (Larson and Richards, 1991), but the extent is much smaller than one-on-one time with mothers.

In addition, we find that fathers report fewer interactive activities when with their adolescent children than do mothers. Specifically, they report less conversation. If we look at the times when both said they were together, we find that the activities fathers report were usually recreational in nature. Compared with mothers, fathers reported more activities in the presence of their children that were leisure: watching TV or active recreation (Figure 1.2; see also Chapter Three of this volume). This leisure focus, I think, follows directly from the description of fathers' lives provided earlier. Fathers exert themselves at their jobs, then come home and claim the right to relax and enjoy themselves.

In sum, these findings indicate that, although fathers spend a substantial amount of time with young adolescent children, this time often involves peripheral interaction, much of it in leisure.

Figure 1.2. Activities Reported by Fathers and Mothers
When Alone with Adolescents

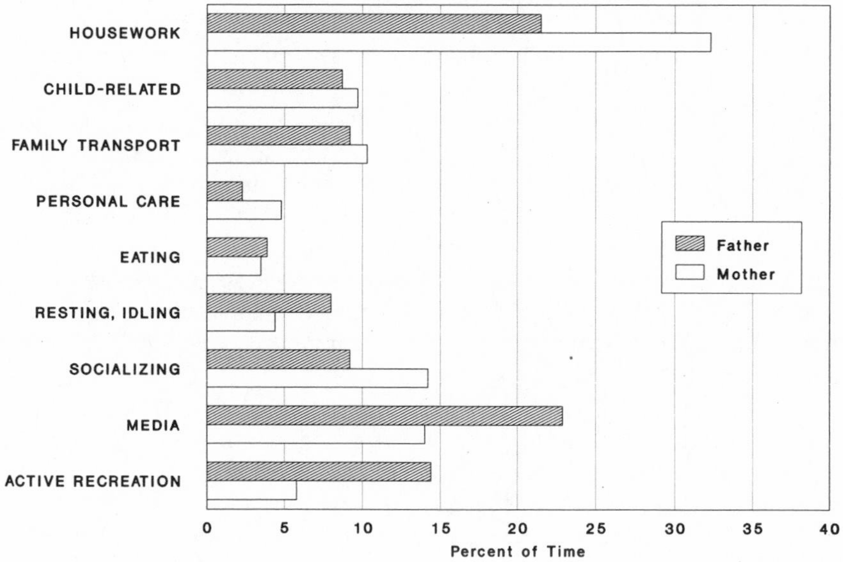

Note: Chi-square $(1,8) = 20.2$, $p = .01$.

An Enjoyment Gap. The next question was, what do fathers and adolescents feel during the times they are together? What are their emotional states? MacDonald (1992) suggests that pleasurable interactions between parent and child are an important evolutionary mechanism that cements mutual investment in parent-child relationships.

To evaluate whether such pleasurable interaction occurs, I focused on only times that both father and adolescent agreed they were together. For each father and adolescent I computed the average score on the affect scale during these occasions. I employed the z-scored values of affect, so the data represent the emotional state relative to the rest of the person's experience. Findings from these analyses showed a substantial difference in what fathers and adolescents reported when they were together.

Fathers' experience in the presence of their young adolescents typically indicated positive affect. Fathers reported average emotional states that were above the mean for the rest of their lives, $(t[34] = 2.08, p = .04)$. This elevation was not evident for mothers. Fathers also reported feeling "kindly" more often when with the adolescent than in other parts of their lives, and they reported feeling "competitive" less often.

Young adolescents, however, did not generally share the fathers' enjoyment of this time. When with fathers, the youths reported being significantly less happy, more competitive, and less kindly compared with their fathers, especially during times when the mother was not present. Furthermore, adolescents' affect with fathers fell as the teen's grade in school increased ($F[3,33]$ = 6.26, p = .02). Older students reported less favorable emotional states in the presence of their fathers, relative to the rest of their lives. It is not that they were markedly unhappy; rather, on average, they were less happy than in other daily contexts.

In short, there was what might be called an "enjoyment gap" between fathers and adolescents that widened between fifth and eighth grades (Figure 1.3). It was evident with boys and with girls, though in father-daughter interactions both parties reported lower affect compared with father-son interactions (Larson and Richards, in press).

One explanation for this gap lies in the relative place of family time in fathers' and adolescents' lives. We found that men's happiest times were in the home sphere, because this is their time of respite from work. In fact, fathers sometimes reported that they were happy when with their children because of the reprieve they were getting from work. Given that men's activities in this situation were often recreational, it is not surprising that they reported comparatively positive emotions. Adolescents, in contrast, report that their happiest times are with friends, and this becomes more consistent with age (Larson and Richards, 1991). Thus, even though they too report a high frequency of leisure activities at home, their mean affect when with the family and with their fathers is comparatively lower.

Figure 1.3. Affect When Fathers and Adolescents Are Together

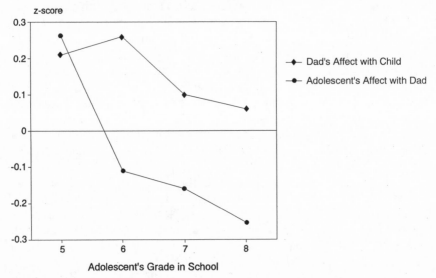

Note: The graph displays the mean means for fathers and adolescents for whom there were at least two times when they agreed they were together.

Another explanation lies in the asymmetry within father-adolescent inter-actions. Fathers have more status and power in the relationship than do ado-lescents (Youniss, 1980). Fathers are often more demanding, dominating, rigid, and threatening than mothers (Lamb, 1981; Paikoff and Brooks-Gunn, 1991). In our study adolescents and fathers concurred in identifying the father as more often being "the leader" when they were together. Fathers never identi-fied the adolescent as being the leader. Given the father's comparative power, it may not be surprising that fathers find these times more gratifying. They control the agenda.

Reflecting on this finding, one of our research assistants recalled an inci-dent from his own youth that is a useful illustration. His father had induced him to go fishing. He remembers sitting in the front of the boat, feeling bored, and wishing he was with his friends. Then his dad turned to him with enthu-siasm and said, "Isn't this great!" In our ESM data similar situations involved a dad taking his daughter to a party with his coworkers and a father razzing his son for not competing hard enough with him in a racquetball game.

The dominance of the father's agenda was also evident in our finding that fathers were unaware of their adolescents' feelings. In their interactions, we asked fathers to "guess" how their son or daughter was rating his or her level of happiness. These guesses bore little relationship to what the child reported. Fathers typically guessed that adolescents were happier than the adolescents reported themselves to be (t[322] = 5.41, p < .001). Whereas mothers had a modest success rate in guessing their adolescents' happiness (r[443] = .25, p < .001), fathers' guesses were no better than chance (r[322] = .02). The telling finding is that the fathers' guesses were correlated with their own level of happiness (r[542] = .32, p < .001). This finding is consistent with other research suggesting that fathers are not very sensitive to adolescents' inner world (Noller and Callan, 1991; Youniss and Smollar, 1985). In their desire to have fun, fathers either were not told, could not see, or did not want to know what was really going on with their sons and daughters. Their own agenda appeared to take priority.

Fathers see themselves as the leaders of these interactions, and they assume that their children are having as much fun as they are. But for adoles-cents life is elsewhere; with age, time with their fathers becomes less enjoyable. This increasing gap in enjoyment, however, is not the critical factor in alien-ation between adolescents and fathers.

Enjoyment Is Not Equal to Warmth. My underlying assumption was that positive affect was desirable and that a good relationship between father and adolescent was one in which they experienced pleasure in being together. I assumed that relationships in which fathers and adolescents reported nega-tive affect together would be less warm. This hypothesis comes from literature on marriage, which shows that distressed marriages are characterized by fre-quent experience of negative emotion in each other's presence (Gottman, 1979; Schaap, 1984). Indeed, our data corroborated this research: husbands and wives who reported more negative affect when together, experienced their relationship as less warm (Larson and Richards, in press).

For father-adolescent relationships, however, the hypothesis was not borne out. If anything, the opposite seemed to be true. For each father and adolescent I computed an average warmth score and an average affect score for the time they were together. Then I examined the correlations between these scores. As Table 1.1 shows, all the correlations between warmth and affect variables are negative. If both reported more positive average affect when together, they rated the relationship as less warm. These correlations are not significant, except for one, but the contrast with expectation is striking. Experiencing more positive affect with each other is not related to a warmer relationship and may even be associated with a colder one. The counterintuitive direction of these trends is further suggested by the negative correlation between affect when together and the adolescents' reported self-esteem as rated on the Rosenberg (1965) scale.

Thus feeling happy together was associated with, if anything, less warmth and lower adolescent self-esteem. And experiencing negative affect in each other's presence was associated with greater warmth and adolescent self-esteem. This direction of association was not evident between adolescents and mothers. Of course, it should be emphasized that these suggested relationships are conditioned by the pool of families in the study. Although the sample included a normative range of families, there were no cases where violent negative affect was reported between father and adolescent. It is fathers and adolescents who experience, not extreme anger, but sadness and mild anger, who are reporting the warmer relations.

The question is, what was going on in these warmer adolescent-father relationships? One of these fathers described how his daughter snaps at him: "In the morning she's one of the crabbiest persons." He said this gets him angry. Another father in a warm relationship with his daughter described an interaction in which he yelled at her to "shut the radio off." The result was: "She blew her cork and that made me mad." These incidents seem to reflect the kind of cycle of negative affect identified in the marital interaction literature as proto-

Table 1.1. Correlation of Warmth with Affect Experienced by Fathers and Adolescents When Together

	Affect When Together	
	Adolescent	Father
Warmth felt		
By adolescent (to father)	$r = -.18, p = .254$	$r = -.14, p = .398$
By father (to adolescent)	$r = -.31, p = .045$	$r = -.16, p = .301$
Adolescent's self-esteem	$r = -.32, p = .036$	$r = -.44, p = .004$

typic of a distressed marriage, and yet they appear to be associated with warmer father-adolescent relationships. Why?

Convenient Exit. An explanation for this puzzling finding was suggested by analyses of the hour-to-hour sequence of father-adolescent interactions. To conduct these analyses, I examined occasions when adolescents and their fathers were together and both responded to a second ESM report within the subsequent four-hour period. Father and adolescent affects at time 1 were the independent variables; their reports of whether they were together at time 2 was the dependent variable. Analyses were conducted separately for colder and warmer father-adolescent pairs, defined by a median split on the adolescents' combined warmth scores.

What these analyses showed was that, for colder pairs, the emotional state that each person reports predicts whether they will be together the next time they are signaled (Figure 1.4). If dad was in a bad mood, they were somewhat less likely to be together at the next beep. If the adolescent was in a bad mood at time 1, they were much less likely to be together at time 2. These correlations were less evident for warmer father-adolescent pairs and for warm or cold mother-adolescent pairs.

This suggests that there is a selection process governing when they are together. If their moods are not positive, father and adolescent separate. This selection process suggests an answer to why fathers and adolescents in colder relationships report more positive affect when together: positive affect is a precondition for being together.

In the individual instances that I examined, a father's insensitivity or expression of anger was often a part of the scenario. Several fathers admitted that they could not handle their daughters' tears; it seems plausible that their daughters, reading this intolerance, felt compelled to separate themselves from their dads. On other occasions, fathers' cross words were a factor. For example, an adolescent reports separating from his dad after a report in which he indicated that his father was yelling at him because he did not want to hear the adolescent's ideas on how the basketball hoop should be hung.

The data also showed that, after separating, the adolescent often reported being in his or her room. This suggests that it is more often the child who physically withdraws from the interaction, though it is possible that his or her physical withdrawal is a response to the father's discomfort, expression of anger, or emotional withdrawal. Since many fathers see their participation at home as voluntary, if father and adolescent are not having fun together, they separate.

Discussion: Father-Adolescent Relationships in Context

The findings reported here should be seen as tentative. The sample size is small, and the significance levels are marginal. Since we do not have data from younger children or older adolescents, it is difficult to determine whether these

Figure 1.4. Father-Adolescent Interactions: Prediction of Being Together at Time 2 by Affect at Time 1

ADOLESCENT <u>DOES NOT</u> FEEL WARM TOWARD FATHER

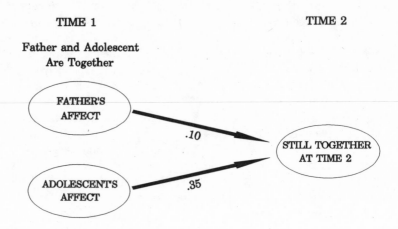

ADOLESCENT <u>DOES</u> FEEL WARM TOWARD FATHER

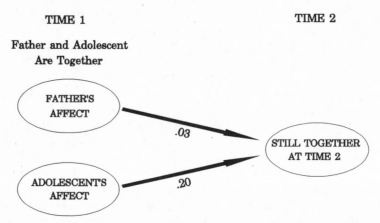

Note: Point biserial correlations shown are based on beep-level analyses. Being together is defined as both saying they are together.

findings are unique to a specific age period, or whether they are general conditions of child-parent relationships. Obviously, no generalizations should be made from these findings outside the limited population of two-parent, European-American families studied here.

What these findings suggest is that alienation between father and adolescent results in part from the structure of the fathers' daily lives. Men come home from work with a double agenda: (1) to relax, enjoy themselves, and recuperate from their exertions as the primary provider at work and (2) to spend time with their families. Our data suggest that they resolve this double agenda by being a partner or leader in leisure activities: watching TV, playing games, or going on outings with their children.

The term "Disneyland Dad" has been coined to describe the recreational nature of divorced, noncustodial fathers' interactions with their children, but the pattern is also evident for fathers who live with their children. When our fathers described their relationships with their adolescent children, they talked a lot about joking and good humor: there seemed to be more emphasis on having a good time in father-adolescent relationships than in mother-adolescent relationships (Larson and Richards, in press). Indeed, fathers often reported that they enjoyed themselves during interactions with their adolescent children. Searching for words, one father said that good times with his children were almost like the times when he gets together with his friends over beers. The reason for this recreational emphasis, I believe, is that, after a day of working hard for the family at their jobs, fathers want to combine their desire to be with their children and their felt need for leisure.

But the findings suggest that, in playing this role, fathers may be missing the boat. First, their adolescent children are not enjoying these interactions as much as they are. Adolescents have their own agenda; their lives and the significance of their families to them are changing, and they obtain fun from the part of their lives spent with peers. By setting enjoyment as the standard, men may be missing what is most valued by adolescents. Second, even when adolescents enjoy this time, it does not create closeness with their fathers. Fathers with whom adolescents have a good time are not those with whom they feel warm. Even when the Disneyland Dads succeed in creating enjoyment in their children, they are not experienced as close (see Asmussen and Larson, 1991).

Some authors have suggested that the most common issue in mother-child relationships is autonomy: avoiding over-enmeshment. Perhaps the main issue in father-child relationships is the opposite: tolerating each other's negative affect, being able to be angry, sad, or depressed with each other without leaving the room. We have seen that many fathers have a relationship with their adolescent children centered on recreation with the goal of having fun. These findings suggest that warm father-adolescent relationships are ones in which being together is less contingent on sharing good times. Our data provide the intriguing suggestion that it is those fathers who can tolerate negative emotion in their adolescents who are experienced as warm. It may be those who can share time with their children, even when fun is not being had, that are more effective as parents.

The bottom line is that many fathers still see parenting as discretionary. They relate to their adolescent children on their own terms; if the father had a bad day at work or if things are not going well with the child, father and adolescent often separate. Sometimes the father's anger triggers a separation; sometimes the father simply opts out. Because of the demands in their lives, fathers are unable or unwilling to compromise their own needs for those of the adolescent.

Yet with the rate of women's employment continuing to increase, many families need and expect fathers to share more household responsibilities, including those of parenting. Strangers in the home only a generation ago, fathers now need to develop means of relating to their children that are more sensitive and empathic.

Future Perspectives: Recreating Fatherhood

Family researchers tell us that we are rapidly moving toward a society in which the family takes many diverse forms, including single-parent families, shared-custody families, and families whose interactions are structured by ethnic traditions. This means that fatherhood too is taking many diverse forms. In this article I have described fatherhood in a single family type: European-American, middle- and working-class, two-parent families. Yet, given this increased diversity, what we need most is information on the many ways in which relations between fathers and adolescents are enacted. Research on how fatherhood is structured in different types of families is valuable, both because each variation is important in its own right and because together these variations provide a richer glossary of knowledge on how families solve the challenges of life together.

Among these challenges, I have argued that a central one is how families structure the daily lives of father, mother, and adolescent in a way that makes for meaningful interactions. The members of any family face a unique array of pressures and opportunities. For parents who are sole breadwinners (whether male or female), a tightening job market and historical declines in wages over the last twenty years mean increased pressure at work. The decline in traditional role expectations may also mean that they receive less support and acknowledgement at home for their breadwinning. For all employed parents, the issue of how one accomplishes the emotional transition from work to home is an important one. We found that many family conflicts occur in the period from 5:00 to 7:00 P.M., when supper needs to be cooked and everyone is arriving home with pressing needs. Future research needs to identify parents, across diverse cultural groups and family arrangements, who have found successful ways to manage this difficult transitional time.

Although there are signs that our society is moving toward more androgynous family roles, I believe it would be wrong not to try to understand how gender differences shape the current family. We might begin by asking what skills men possess that can be developed to make them warmer and more responsive parents to their adolescents. Stuart Hauser and colleagues (1991) found that, at least in a lab situation, fathers interact with their adolescent children in a way that promotes the adolescents' independence. Compared with mothers, they make more statements that encourage teens to take a personal point of view and they often help teens focus on thinking through a problem from their vantage point. We might ask, can these skills be supported and developed within daily interactions? How can men redirect their disposition to leadership in the best interest of the child?

Recently efforts have been made to develop interventions and training programs to help fathers of preschool children be more involved and responsive. Because these programs address the specific issues of fathers, such as their stress from work and their socialization as males, these programs have proved to be quite successful (Hawkins and Roberts, 1992; McBride, 1990, 1991; Roberts, Hawkins, and Marshall, 1992). The time is ripe for such programs to be developed and tested for the particular issues of father-adolescent relationships. By all evidence, the skills needed to be a sensitive parent are not innate; they are learned by both men and women (Daniels and Weingarten, 1988). Anthropologists have found cultures where fathers are tender and nurturant (Harris, 1983; Katz and Konner, 1981). The task is now to find ways for fathers in our cultural milieu to develop this kind of warm parenting.

In the case of John Niles, the detrimental effect that his job was having on his family became increasingly apparent to him, so he switched to a job with less pressure. He also joined Alcoholics Anonymous to seek help for his drinking, which had become out of control. His wife began going to school to develop her career, a change that required him to put more time into the family. John still plays the Disneyland Dad; during the week of the ESM study, he took Luke to a movie and brought him along when he went to buy a motorcycle. But John is also frequently the parent who is there when Luke comes home from school. He helps Luke with his homework, and Luke says he often goes to his father for advice, even about his friendships. Both describe the relationship as warmer and much improved. Because John now brings less stress from his job, and because of a change in attitude, he is now more emotionally flexible and available to his adolescent child.

References

Asmussen, L., and Larson, R. "The Quality of Family Time Among Young Adolescents in Single-Parent and Married-Parent Families." Journal of Marriage and the Family, 1991, 53, 1021– 1030.

Bernard, J. "The Good-Provider Role." American Psychologist, 1981, 36, 1–12.

Blyth, D. A. "Mapping the Social World of Adolescents: Issues, Techniques, and Problems." In F. Serafica (ed.), Social Cognition, Context, and Social Behavior: A Developmental Perspective. New York: Guilford Press, 1982.

Collins, W. A., and Russell, G. "Mother-Child and Father-Child Relationships in Middle Childhood and Adolescence: A Developmental Analysis." Developmental Review, 1991, 11, 99–136.

Crouter, A. C., Perry-Jenkins, M., Huston, T. L., and Crawford, D. W. "The Influence of Work-Induced Psychological States on Behavior at Home." Basic and Applied Social Psychology, 1989, 10 (3), 273–292.

Csikszentmihalyi, M., and Larson, R. "The Experience Sampling Method." Journal of Nervous and Mental Disease, 1987, 175, 526–536.

Daniels, P., and Weingarten, K. "The Fatherhood Click: The Timing of Parenthood in Men's Lives." In P. Bronstein and C. P. Cowan (eds.), Fatherhood Today: Men's Changing Role in the Family. New York: Wiley, 1988.

Demos, J. "The Changing Faces of Fatherhood: A New Exploration in American Family History." In S. H. Cath, A. R. Gurwith, and J. M. Ross (eds.), Father and Child. Boston: Little, Brown, 1982.

Dix, T. "The Affective Organization of Parenting: Adaptive and Maladaptive Processes." Psychological Bulletin, 1991, 110, 3–25.

Gecas, V. "The Socialization and Child Care Roles." In F. I. Nye (ed.), Role Structure and Analysis of the Family. Newbury Park, Calif.: Sage, 1976.

Gjerde, P. F. "The Interpersonal Structure of Family Interaction Settings: Parent-Adolescent Relations in Dyads and Triads." Developmental Psychology, 1986, 22, 297–304.

Goodman, D. A Parents' Guide to the Emotional Needs of Children. New York: Hawthorn Books, 1959.

Gottman, J. M. Marital Interaction: Experimental Investigations. New York: Academic Press, 1979.

Gottman, J. M. "Predicting the Longitudinal Course of Marriages." Journal of Marital and Family Therapy, 1991, 17 (1), 3–7.

Gottman, J. M., and Levenson, R. W. "Assessing the Role of Emotion in Marriage." Behavioral Assessment, 1986, 8, 31–48.

Hareven, T. Family Time and Industrial Time. New York: Cambridge Press, 1982.

Harris, O. "Heavenly Fathers." In U. Owen (ed.), Fathers: Reflections by Daughters. New York: Pantheon, 1983.

Hauser, S. T. (with Powers, S. I., and Noam, G. G.). Adolescents and Their Families: Paths of Ego Development. New York: Free Press, 1991.

Hawkins, A. J., and Roberts, T. A. "Designing a Primary Intervention to Help Dual-Earner Couples Share Housework and Child Care." Family Relations, 1992, 41 (5), 169–177.

Hood, J. C. "The Provider Role: Its Meaning and Measurement. Journal of Marriage and the Family, 1986, 48, 349–359.

Jahoda, M. Employment and Unemployment. Cambridge: Cambridge Press, 1982.

Johannis, T. B., Jr. "Participation by Fathers, Mothers and Teenage Sons and Daughters in Selected Child Care and Control Activity." The Coordinator, 1957, 6 (2), 31–32.

Katz, B. How to Be a Better Parent. New York: Ronald Press, 1953.

Katz, M. M., and Konner, M. J. "The Role of the Father: An Anthropological Perspective." In M. E. Lamb (ed.), The Role of the Father in Child Development. New York: Wiley, 1981.

Lamb, M. E. "Fathers and Child Development: An Integrative Overview." In M. E. Lamb (ed.), The Role of the Father in Child Development. New York: Wiley, 1981.

Lamb, M. E., "Introduction: The Emergent American Father." In M. E. Lamb (ed.), The Father's Role: Cross-Cultural Perspectives. Hillsdale, N.J.: Erlbaum, 1987.

Larson, R. W. "Social Contexts of Adolescents: A World unto Themselves." Illinois Research, 1988, 30 (2), 6–9.

Larson, R. W. "Beeping Children and Adolescents: A Method for Studying Time Use and Daily Experience." Journal of Youth and Adolescence, 1989a, 18, 511–530.

Larson, R. W. The Factor Structure of Moods and Emotions in a Sample of Young Adolescents. Champaign: University of Illinois Press, 1989b.

Larson, R. W., and Asmussen, L. "Anger, Worry, and Hurt in Early Adolescence: An Enlarging World of Negative Emotions." In M. E. Colton and S. Gore (eds.), Adolescent Stress, Social Relationships, and Mental Health. Hawthorne, N.Y.: Aldine de Gruyter, 1991.

Larson, R. W., and Ham, M. "Stress and 'Storm and Stress' in Early Adolescence." Developmental Psychology, 1993, 29 (1), 130–140.

Larson, R. W., and Richards, M. H. (eds.). "The Changing Life Space of Early Adolescence." (special issue) Journal of Youth and Adolescence, 1989, 18 (6).

Larson, R. W., and Richards, M. H. "Daily Companionship in Late Childhood and Early Adolescence: Changing Developmental Contexts." Child Development, 1991, 62, 284–300.

Larson, R. W., and Richards. M. H. Divergent Realities: The Emotional Lives of Young Adolescents, Their Mothers and Fathers. New York: Basic Books, in press.

Lein, L. "Male Participation in Home Life: Impact of Social Supports and Breadwinner Responsibility on the Allocation of Tasks." *Family Coordinator*, 1979, *28*, 489–495.

Levinson, D. J. *The Seasons of a Man's Life*. New York: Ballantine Books, 1978.

McBride, B. A. "The Effects of a Parent Education/Play Group Program on Father Involvement in Child Rearing." *Family Relations*, 1990, *39*, 250–256.

McBride, B. A. "Parental Support Programs and Paternal Stress: An Exploratory Study." *Early Childhood Research Quarterly*, 1991, *6*, 137–149.

MacDonald, K. "Warmth as a Developmental Construct: An Evolutionary Analysis." *Child Development*, 1992, *63* (4), 753–773.

Noller, P., and Callan, V. *The Adolescent in the Family*. New York: Routledge, 1991.

Paikoff, R. L., and Brooks-Gunn, J. "Do Parent-Child Relationships Change During Puberty?" *Psychological Bulletin*, 1991, *110*, 47–66.

Perry-Jenkins, M., and Crouter, A. C. "Men's Provider-Role Attitudes: Implications for Household Work and Marital Satisfaction." *Journal of Family Issues*, 1990, *11*, 136–156.

Pleck, J. H. "Two Worlds in One." *Journal of Social History*, 1976, *10*, 178–195.

Pleck, J. H. *Working Wives/Working Husbands*. Newbury Park, Calif.: Sage, 1985.

Pleck, J. H. "Employment and Fatherhood: Issues and Innovative Policies." In M. E. Lamb (ed.), *The Father Role: Applied Perspectives*. New York: Wiley, 1986.

Repetti, R. L. "Effects of Daily Workload on Subsequent Behavior During Marital Interaction: The Roles of Social Withdrawal and Spouse Support." *Journal of Personality and Social Psychology*, 1989, *57* (4), 651–659.

Roberts, R. A., Hawkins, A. J., and Marshall, C. " A Multi-Method Evaluation of a Program to Help Dual-Earner Couples Share Housework and Child Care." Paper presented at the 54th annual conference of the National Council on Family Relations, Orlando, Fla., November 1992.

Rosenberg, M. *Society and the Adolescent Self-Image*. Princeton, N.J.: Princeton University Press, 1965.

Schaap, C. "A Comparison of the Interaction of Distressed and Nondistressed Married Couples in a Laboratory Situation: Literature Survey, Methodological Issues, and an Empirical Investigation." In K. Hahlweg and N. Jacobson (eds.), *Marital Interaction: Analysis and Modification*. New York: Guilford Press, 1984.

Stafford, F. P., and Duncan, G. J. "The Use of Time and Technology by Households in the United States." In F. T. Juster and F. P. Stafford (eds.), *Time, Goods, and Well-Being*. Ann Arbor, Mich.: Institute for Social Research, 1985.

Steinberg, L., and Silverberg, S. B. "The Vicissitudes of Autonomy in Early Adolescence." *Child Development*, 1986, *57*, 841–851.

Youniss, J. *Parents and Peers in Social Development*. Chicago: University of Chicago Press, 1980.

Youniss, J., and Ketterlinus, R. D. "Communication and Connectedness in Mother- and Father-Adolescent Relationships." *Journal of Youth and Adolescence*, 1987, *16*, 265–280.

Youniss, J., and Smollar, J. *Adolescent Relations with Mothers, Fathers, and Friends*. Chicago: University of Chicago Press, 1985.

REED W. LARSON *is professor and chair of the Division of Human Development and Family Studies at the University of Illinois in Urbana-Champaign.*

Over a period of two and one-half years, father-adolescent relations remained relatively stable in rank-order, but mean levels of child care, acceptance, and conflict decreased. These results imply changing functions of fathers in the lives of adolescents.

Continuity and Change in Father-Adolescent Relations

David M. Almeida, Nancy L. Galambos

Developmental psychologists commonly assume that parent-child relations change as a function of the age of the child. For example, Maccoby (1980) argued that "the development of the child is a powerful force, enabling or even requiring parents and children to take on new joint agendas and to adapt increasingly to new forms of interaction with each other" (p. 326). Such changes may reflect a shift from unilateral authority and regulation of child by parent toward a system of coregulation between parent and child (Maccoby, 1984). Early in a child's development, parent-child interactions are likely to revolve around doing things for the child (for example, changing, feeding, bathing). As the child develops, these interactions shift toward doing things with the child (for example, playing games, doing chores, helping with homework). During adolescence, pronounced biological, psychological, and social transformations are likely to herald changes in parent-child relations.

Despite these speculations regarding developmental changes in parent-adolescent relations, relatively little research has examined such changes longitudinally. Even fewer studies have addressed changes in *father*-adolescent relations across time. To date, most research has focused on either younger children (Roberts, Block, and Block, 1984) or mothers (McNally, Eisenberg, and Harris, 1991). Thus empirical evidence regarding change in father-adolescent relations has been inferred either from studies using cross-sectional data obtained from fathers or their adolescent children or from longitudinal

This research was conducted through Social Sciences and Humanities Research Council of Canada and University of Victoria Faculty Research grants to N. Galambos. We thank the families in this study for their continuing participation.

studies of mother-adolescent relations. Although these approaches can provide a foundation for predicting changes in father-adolescent relations, the only way to examine these changes is to follow over time a group of fathers and adolescents. Accordingly, in this study we examined the trajectories of several aspects of father-adolescent relations, using the reports of fathers and adolescents who participated in a two-and-one-half-year longitudinal study, beginning when the adolescents were in sixth grade. To assess change, we examined both continuity (that is, rank-order stability) and mean-level change in the father's involvement in child-care responsibilities, the level of acceptance and conflict between fathers and adolescents, and the discrepancy between fathers' and adolescents' reports of father acceptance.

Our exploration of how father-adolescent relations changed over time assumed the usefulness of considering the multiple ways in which fathers and adolescents interact. This multidimensional approach implies that, for the description of any particular relationship, several domains of the relationship should be considered. A multidimensional approach not only provides a more complete picture of father-adolescent relations but also allows us to compare and contrast the varied ways in which fathers and adolescents interact. In addition, a multidimensional approach is informative in the initial phases of describing a particular relationship. As previously mentioned, knowledge about fathers and their adolescents is often inferred from studies of how mothers and adolescents interact. Casting a wider net by examining multiple dimensions of father-adolescent relations will point to similarities and differences in the ways that mothers and fathers interact with their adolescents, and it will lead us to determine whether it might be important to study further particular aspects of father-adolescent relations. Thus we hope to provide a framework for examining multiple aspects simultaneously. In this regard, Collins and Russell (1991) discussed three dimensions along which father-adolescent relations might change: quantity of interaction, quality of interaction, and interpersonal perceptions of the relationship.

Changes in the Quantity of Interactions

Changes in the amount of time and the frequency with which fathers and adolescents interact may reflect adolescents' increasing autonomy. As children become more involved in relations and experiences outside of the family, the opportunities for interactions between fathers and adolescents might diminish. In a cross-sectional study, DeLuccie and Davis (1991) found that fathers of sixteen-year-olds were less involved in child care (in terms of the frequency of caregiving, recreational involvement, and school-related involvement) than fathers of eight-year-olds or fathers of four-year-olds. Montemayor and Brownlee (1987) found that older adolescents (grades eight to twelve) reported spending less time with their fathers than younger adolescents (grades six and seven). These findings are consistent with other studies showing a general decrease in adolescents' participation in family activities during early and middle adolescence (Csikszentmihalyi and Larson, 1984; Hill and others, 1985a, 1985b). These studies led us to consider the father's level of involvement in child-care responsibilities across early adolescence.

Changes in the Quality of Interactions

Qualitative aspects of father-adolescent interactions may also change during adolescence. Relations between fathers and adolescents tend to be positive and remain so during the adolescent years (Hill, 1987; Steinberg, 1990). At the same time, fathers' expression of affect and control seem to vary with the age of the adolescent. For example, DeLuccie and Davis's (1991) cross-sectional study found that fathers of preschoolers (age four) were more accepting of their children than fathers of school-age children (age eight) or fathers of adolescents (age sixteen), based on fathers' self-reported parental behaviors. There were no age differences in psychological control or expressions of firm discipline. Fathers of adolescent children, however, felt more satisfied with their parenting performance than fathers of younger children. Higher parenting satisfaction among fathers of older children may be indicative of increasing mutuality between parents and adolescents (Grotevant and Cooper, 1985).

The level of father-adolescent conflict (such as disagreements and bickering) is another qualitative aspect of father-adolescent relationships that may change during early adolescence. Many people believe that conflicts between parents and adolescents peak during early adolescence and then decline (Montemayor, 1983). Some cross-sectional studies have supported this notion (Clark-Lempers, Lempers, and Ho, 1991; Steinberg and Hill, 1978), but others have not (Smetana, 1989). Findings from longitudinal studies are also inconsistent with respect to change in parent-adolescent conflict during early adolescence. Steinberg (1989) found that pubertal maturation during early adolescence was associated with increases in father-daughter conflict over the span of one year. In contrast, parent-adolescent conflict over household chores, appearance, and politeness decreased between the ages of eleven and one-half and fourteen (Galambos and Almeida, 1992). Given the interest in both positive and negative affect in father-adolescent relations, we focused in our study on the level of father acceptance toward the adolescent and the level of conflict between them.

Changes in Interpersonal Perceptions of Father-Adolescent Relations

Interpersonal perceptions of father-adolescent relations—the difference in how fathers and adolescents each view their relationship (Collins and Russell, 1991)—may also change over time, with increasing congruence to be expected in some domains. Such changes might be the result of the adolescent's increasing social-cognitive abilities. Indeed, Alessandri and Wozniak (1987) found that older adolescents more accurately perceived their fathers' beliefs about them than did preadolescents. The results of a two-year follow-up study of these children and their parents showed that, in the younger group, the congruence in perception between fathers and their children significantly increased over the two years (Alessandri and Wozniak, 1989). The older group of adolescents, however, did not change in their awareness of their fathers' beliefs about their behavior. These findings suggest that the period of early adolescence may be a time of change in cognitive markers of father-child relations and that by later adolescence this change may have stabilized.

Additional evidence of possible changes in perspectives on father-adolescent relations is provided by Smetana's (1989) study of adolescents' and parents' perceptions of parental authority. In this study of fifth through twelfth graders, the number of moral, social, and personal issues that adolescents viewed as falling under their own jurisdiction increased with age; parents, however, continued to view many issues as falling under parental control. Thus the mismatch between adolescents' and parents' views was wider with each adolescent age group. At the same time, however, older adolescents (grade twelve) and parents recognized each other's opinions more than younger adolescents and their parents. Thus Smetana's work implies that many adolescents and fathers disagree with each other's point of view but are aware of the other's opinions. Our data allowed us to examine the difference in perspective between adolescents and fathers regarding father acceptance.

Taken together, the small number of studies of age-related differences and change in father-adolescent relations points to possible transformations in the quantitative, qualitative, and perceptual dimensions of these relations. However, the picture is just beginning to emerge. Longitudinal data are needed to address the issue of continuity and change in fathers' and adolescents' impressions of their relationship. Furthermore, no single study has examined simultaneously changes in the quantity, quality, and interpersonal perceptions of father-adolescent relations. The present study adds to the existing knowledge by observing these three aspects of father-adolescent relations across two and one-half years during early adolescence. We examined both rank-order stability and mean-level change in the measures of the father-adolescent relationship. This longitudinal and multidimensional focus represents an important step forward by synthesizing a diverse set of research findings and painting a more complete picture of change in father-adolescent relations.

Method

Participants. The subjects were adolescents and their fathers who participated in a longitudinal study of two-parent families in which both parents were employed (N = 112—60 girls and 52 boys). The sample consisted primarily of white working- and middle-class families with an average of 2.4 children. Fathers were, on average, 40 years old with 13.8 years of education. The mean number of years that the parents were married was 14.7, and in eight couples one or both of the spouses reported being remarried. In terms of marriage and employment, the families were highly stable. The sample and procedures are described in further detail elsewhere (Galambos and Almeida, 1992; Galambos and Maggs, 1991).

Data collection began in the winter of 1988 (time 1), when the adolescents were in sixth grade (mean age = 11.6 years; SD = 5 months), and continued on three more occasions: the summer after sixth grade (time 2), the winter of seventh grade (time 3), and the summer after eighth grade (time 4). Adolescents made the transition from elementary school (K–7) between seventh and eighth grades, with about two-thirds going to middle schools (grades eight to ten) and the rest going to high schools (grades eight to twelve).

Procedure. The sample was obtained through letters sent home with sixth graders in a medium-sized Canadian city and through advertisements run in local newspapers. Criteria for participation were that the household contained two parents (not necessarily biological parents) who were employed (that is, they identified themselves as having jobs) and that both parents and the adolescent wanted to participate. Questionnaires were mailed to each parent and child individually. Family members were instructed not to discuss the questionnaires and were given separate return envelopes. Each family member received a token payment for completing the questionnaire. Of the 112 families who initially participated at time 1, 90 percent returned the second questionnaire, 82 percent returned the third, and 62 percent returned the fourth. Comparisons of adolescents and fathers who participated at all four times with those who participated at time 1 but did not participate at time 4 revealed no differences between the groups on demographic characteristics (mother and father education, mother and father age, mother and father occupational status, and number of children), father-adolescent relations, or indexes of father and adolescent psychological health. The one exception was that fathers who dropped out of the study reported higher job-family role strain at time 1 (t = 2.00, p < .05). None of the families who remained in the study reported becoming divorced or separated during the study period.

Cases for the present investigation were selected on the basis of their pattern of missing data across time. Father-adolescent dyads were included in which (1) either father or adolescent participated on all four occasions and (2) both father and adolescent participated on at least three of the four occasions. Seventy-one father-adolescent dyads met these criteria. Still, the longitudinal pattern for some of these fathers and adolescents included missing data. Because the pattern of missing data was random (that is, there was no systematic pattern of nonresponse), it was appropriate to estimate scores (see Little and Rubin, 1987). Estimated scores were generated for the nine fathers and five adolescents who had some missing data. Scores for missing data were estimated by weighting the group mean of the given variable for the individual on that occasion by the subject's average deviation from the group mean at the other complete data points. This method was performed separately for families of adolescent girls and families of boys. This procedure resulted in complete data for seventy-one father-adolescent dyads. The means and standard deviations of this subsample were comparable to those for subjects present on any given occasion.

Measures. Data for the present study consisted of adolescent and father reports obtained on four occasions. Measures assessed quantity, quality, and interpersonal perceptions of father-adolescent relations.

Quantity of Interaction: Child-Care Composite. Quantity of interaction was assessed by a composite of two measures: child-care frequency and child-care hours. The child-care frequency measure was derived from a family task-sharing scale (Bird, Bird, and Scruggs, 1984). Fathers indicated from "never" (1) to "every day" (5) the frequency with which they (1) performed daily care of children, (2) chauffeured children, and (3) attended functions with children (Almeida and Galambos, 1991). Mean scores were computed in which higher scores represented more frequent participation in child-care tasks. The internal consistency for the child-care frequency items ranged from .58 to .70 across the four times of measurement.

The child-care hours measure was from Pleck's (1985) analysis of the Quality of Employment Survey. Each father was asked to estimate how much time, in hours, he spent on working and nonworking days "taking care of and doing things with your child(ren)." Hours per week were derived by summing workday and nonworkday estimates, appropriately weighted by each father's number of workdays or nonworkdays per week. Pleck (1985) found that this self-reported index was comparable to observer estimates of the level of child care reported in other studies.

Child-care frequency and hours were aggregated to form a composite measure. The measures were standardized before being combined. To maintain mean-level differences across time, deviations from the grand mean (that is, the average of the scores across the times of measurement) were computed and divided by the averaged across-time standard deviation. The composite score consisted of the mean of these two standardized scores. At time 4, this composite demonstrated a high degree of overlap with a seventeen-item scale on frequency of father-adolescent activities (for example, "helped with homework"; $r = .61, p < .001$).

Quality of Interaction: Acceptance and Conflict. The quality of father-adolescent interactions was measured based on fathers' expressions of acceptance (warmth and understanding) toward their adolescents and the level of father-adolescent conflict.

The acceptance subscale of the fifty-six–item version (Armentrout and Burger, 1972) of the Children's Report of Parental Behavior Inventory (CRPBI;) (Schaefer, 1965) was used to assess the degree of warmth and acceptance directed toward the adolescent by the father. The acceptance subscale consists of the mean of twenty-four items (for example, "I always speak to my child with a warm and friendly voice"), with responses ranging from "very much unlike me" (1) to "very much like me" (5). The adolescents completed the subscale about their fathers' behavior; the fathers rated the same twenty-four items with respect to their own behavior toward their adolescent children. Higher scores indicated higher parental acceptance. The coefficient alpha ranged from .90 to .97 for father and adolescent reports.

The Issues Checklist (Prinz, Foster, Kent, and O'Leary, 1979) was used to measure the level of conflict between fathers and adolescents. This measure listed forty-four topics (for example, cleaning up bedroom), and fathers indicated whether these topics were discussed in the last two weeks. The discussion was rated with possible responses ranging from "very calm" (1) to "very angry" (5). Intensity of conflict was computed based on calculation of the mean level of anger for all topics discussed. Frequency of conflict was computed by summing the number of topics with an intensity of 2 or above (see Steinberg, 1987), The coefficient alpha ranged from .86 to .94 for conflict intensity and frequency across the four times of measurement. The intensity and frequency scores were standardized across time to preserve mean-level differences across time. Composite conflict scores were then computed at each time of measurement based on the mean of the two standardized scores.

Interpersonal Perceptions of Father-Adolescent Relations. Interpersonal perceptions of father-adolescent relations were measured by the discrepancy between fathers' and adolescents' reports of fathers' acceptance as assessed by the acceptance subscale of the CRPBI (Schaefer, 1965). First, discrepancy scores were calculated for each of the twenty-four items based on the absolute value of the difference between the adolescent's response and the father's response. Second, a mean discrepancy score for the twenty-four items was computed. Accordingly, higher discrepancy scores represent a greater absolute difference between adolescents' and fathers' reports of paternal acceptance. The coefficient alpha for this measure ranged from .73 to .89 across the times of measurement.

Results

Table 2.1 displays the means and standard deviations of the individual and composite measures of father-adolescent relations. It is interesting to note that fathers spent an average of fifteen to nineteen hours per week with their children. They also expressed a relatively high level of acceptance toward their adolescents, according to both fathers and adolescents. Fathers also reported

**Table 2.1. Means and Standard Deviations of the Variables
at Each Time of Measurement**

Variable	Time 1 Mean (SD)	Time 2 Mean (SD)	Time 3 Mean (SD)	Time 4 Mean (SD)
Quantity of interaction				
Child-care frequency	—	2.60 (0.99)	2.63 (0.74)	2.22 (0.78)
Child-care hours[a]	—	19.32 (9.89)	18.45 (10.7)	15.09 (7.68)
Child-care composite[b]	—	0.16 (0.94)	0.13 (0.76)	−0.29 (0.68)
Quality of interaction				
Acceptance (F)	3.60 (0.34)	3.59 (0.46)	3.51 (0.38)	3.43 (0.48)
Acceptance (A)	3.74 (0.75)	3.64 (0.68)	3.66 (0.82)	3.59 (0.72)
Conflict intensity	1.90 (0.44)	1.92 (0.43)	0.72 (0.40)	0.79 (0.47)
Conflict frequency	11.86 (7.28)	11.74 (7.92)	8.13 (5.88)	10.14 (7.84)
Conflict composite[c]	0.76 (0.89)	0.81 (0.94)	−0.87 (0.85)	−0.70 (1.05)
Interpersonal perceptions Acceptance (F)				
– Acceptance (A)	1.05 (0.30)	0.92 (0.36)	0.93 (0.43)	1.02 (0.37)

Note: N = 71. F = Father report, A = Adolescent report.

[a] Per week.

[b] Average of across-time standardized child-care frequency and hours scores.

[c] Average of conflict intensity and frequency standardized scores.

that they had, on average, between eight and twelve conflicts with their adolescents in the previous two weeks and that the average intensity of conflicts was relatively low. The acceptance discrepancy measure indicated that adolescents and their fathers deviated by about one point on a five-point scale.

To provide a general picture of the interrelations within and between the three domains of father-adolescent relations (quantity, quality, and interpersonal perceptions), intercorrelations among the father-adolescent relations variables were computed at each time of measurement. Father-adolescent conflict was negatively related to father reports of acceptance at times 1 and 2 ($r = -.42$ and .24, respectively) and to adolescents' reports of acceptance at time 2 ($r = -.20$). At times 2 and 3, a greater discrepancy in interpersonal perceptions of acceptance was associated with lower acceptance and higher conflict ($r = .21$ and .37, respectively). At time 3, a higher child-care composite score was associated with higher father acceptance (as reported by fathers) ($r = .39$).

Rank-Order Stability. One question of interest in examining change over time pertains to the rank-order stability of scores. To assess stability, we computed autocorrelations of the measures of father-adolescent relations for various time lags ranging from six months (for example, time 1 to time 2) to thirty months (time 1 to time 4). These correlations suggest a moderate to high degree of stability for the measures across occasions (r range from .39 to .81, all $p < .01$). The variables for quality of interaction (acceptance and conflict) were, on average, more stable than those for quantity of interaction (child care). On average, the short-term stabilities (that is, stability across adjacent times of measurement) were higher than the longer-term stabilities. These figures indicate that individual differences in aspects of father-adolescent relations are maintained across time.

Mean-Level Change. A series of analyses examined the pattern of mean change in the domains of father-adolescent relations over time. Repeated-measures MANOVAs and follow-up ANOVAs were computed with time as a within-subjects factor and sex of adolescent as a between-subjects factor. Linear and quadratic polynomial contrasts weighted for the unequal interval between time 3 and time 4 (eighteen months) compared with the other adjacent intervals (six months) tested hypotheses about mean-level change over time (Wilkinson, 1988). Because child-care measures were not available at time 1, we assessed mean change in child care in a separate analysis.

The first analysis examined mean change in the child-care composite from time 2 through time 4. The results of this ANOVA showed that involvement in child care decreased over time ($F[2,138] = 13.35$, $p < .001$) with a significant linear trend ($F[1,69] = 20.41$, $p < .001$). The quadratic trend, the sex of adolescent main effect, and the interactions were not significant. The absence of a main effect for sex of adolescent indicated that the level of child care for fathers of sons did not differ significantly from that for fathers of daughters.

The second analysis examined mean changes in the other father-adolescent relations variables from time 1 to time 4 with fathers' report of acceptance, adolescents' report of acceptance, composite conflict, and interpersonal perceptions as the dependent measures. The results showed a significant multivariate main effect for time (Pillais multivariate $F[6,414] = 38.83$, $p < .001$). The univariate tests revealed that fathers' reports of acceptance decreased over time ($F[3,207] = 7.96$, $p < .001$) with a significant linear trend ($F[1,69] = 11.95$, $p < .001$). Adolescent reports of father acceptance, however, did not evidence a significant time effect. The level of father-adolescent conflict also decreased over time ($F[3,207] = 145.39$, $p < .001$) with a significant linear trend ($F[1,69] = 209.63$, $p < .001$). No other effects were significant.

The analysis of mean change in interpersonal perceptions showed a univariate main effect for time ($F[3,207] = 3.84$, $p < .01$) with a significant quadratic trend ($F[1,69] = 10.76$, $p < .01$). The linear and cubic trends were not significant. These results indicated that the discrepancy between fathers' and adolescents' perceptions of father acceptance initially declined and subsequently increased over time.

According to the MANOVA, the multivariate and univariate main effect for sex of adolescent and the interactions were not significant. Thus, father-daughter dyads did not differ significantly from father-son dyads with respect to father and adolescent reports of acceptance, conflict, or interpersonal perceptions.

Discussion

Our analyses provide a descriptive account of changes in several aspects of father-adolescent relations during early adolescence through examining rank-order stability and mean-level change in several aspects of father-adolescent relations. The results for individual differences in the rank ordering of father-adolescent relations across time showed that qualitative aspects of father-adolescent relations (acceptance and conflict) demonstrated relatively high stability even over the two-and-one-half-year interval. For example, fathers who were very accepting remained so. Fathers' quantity of interaction with their adolescents (that is, child care) was less consistent, however. One reason for this difference is that the variables for quality of interaction may reflect more fundamental and enduring child-rearing values, whereas those for quantity of interaction may be indicative of behavioral characteristics that are more dependent on situations and contexts (Roberts, Block, and Block, 1984).

The results of the mean-level change analysis indicated that fathers decreased their level of involvement in child care as their adolescents matured; according to fathers, but not adolescents, fathers' expressions of acceptance decreased over the two and one-half years; and fathers' reports of conflictual interactions also decreased. Other studies of changes in child care have shown a similar trend toward less contact between fathers and adolescents during early adolescence (Montemayor and Brownlee, 1987; DeLuccie and Davis, 1991). As adolescents become more involved in relations outside of the family, the opportunities for interaction with their fathers may diminish.

The findings for fathers' reports of acceptance are consistent with previous longitudinal research on mother-adolescent relations (McNally, Eisenberg, and Harris, 1991) and cross-sectional research on father-adolescent relations (DeLuccie and Davis, 1991). This comparability between mothers and fathers in how relations with their adolescents change is interesting given that fathers typically show less warmth toward their adolescents than do mothers. It appears that both parents express slightly less warmth during their child's early adolescence. It is important to note that in the present study, as in other studies (for example, Deluccie and Davis, 1991), the average level of acceptance remained relatively high throughout adolescence despite this slight decrease. In the present sample, fathers' average level of acceptance was well above the midpoint of the scale at every time of measurement. Furthermore, adolescent reports of father acceptance were consistently higher than father reports of their acceptance, and adolescents' reports of father acceptance did not change significantly over time. Thus it appears that fathers continue to express warmth and acceptance toward their children during adolescence. Rather than being nonsupportive or hostile toward their children, the slight decrease in fathers' reports of acceptance may be indicative of their expectations of more independent and responsible adolescent behavior (Maccoby, 1984; Roberts, Block, and Block, 1984).

The decrease in fathers' reports of conflict (see also Galambos and Almeida, 1992) refute the notion of a general increase in conflictual interactions during early adolescence (Montemayor, 1983). One major difference between the present study and previous studies of parent-adolescent conflict is the use of a longitudinal design. This study of intra-individual change indicates decreases in conflict, whereas studies of interindividual age differences have suggested a somewhat different picture. It may be that decreases in conflict are, in part, due to less frequent interaction between fathers and adolescents. A decrease in the amount of contact may reduce the opportunity for conflict between them. Future longitudinal research should replicate these findings and explore possible mechanisms that might account for increases or decreases in parent-adolescent conflict.

With respect to interpersonal perceptions of father-adolescent relations, over the two and one-half years studied, the absolute discrepancy between fathers' and adolescents' reports of father acceptance initially decreased and then evidenced a slight increase. To a certain degree, these findings are consistent with Alessandri and Wozniak's (1989) contention that early adolescence may be a period marked by cognitive changes in adolescents' perceptions of their familial relations, and after this period of change perceptions may stabilize. In the present study, the discrepancy between fathers' and adolescents' reports of fathers' acceptance decreased between the sixth and seventh grades. However, in the eighteen months that followed, the discrepancy between fathers' and adolescents' reports slightly increased. Smetana (1989) also found an increase over time in the mismatch between adolescents' and parents' views of issues falling under parental authority. In the present study the slight increase in discrepant perceptions of father acceptance may reflect the decrease in father reports of acceptance in combination with the adolescent's unchanging views of father acceptance. Taken together, the mean-level analyses demonstrated that, on average, the relations between fathers and adolescents changed somewhat during early adolescence.

The overall picture of the results addressing change in father-adolescent relations points to both continuity (in terms of rank-order stability) and change (in terms of group means). Change in the quantity and quality of interactions appeared to reflect decreases in provisional care and acceptance, as well as decreases in conflict. This pattern of relationship change may reflect changing functions of fathers in the lives of their adolescent children, from providing basic care to promoting independence and responsibility. At the same time, adolescents may be seeking their own sense of identity and individualism in the family. Grotevant and Cooper (1985) propose that this process involves asserting separateness in the family and at the same time remaining connected to family members. These dual agendas appeared to be evident in the present findings in terms of decreased contact (that is, child-care involvement) and increased connectedness (that is, decreased conflict).

Generalizations of these conclusions should be considered in light of some limitations of the data. First, the participants were fathers and adolescents in two-earner families. The results might differ for employed fathers in single-earner families. Work and family obligations are more likely to conflict for parents in dual-earner families than in two-parent, single-earner families. Such demands may have given fathers in the present sample fewer choices about their level of involvement with their children (that is, they have to be involved to some extent) (Crouter, Perry-Jenkins, Huston, and McHale, 1987), which in turn may have implications for father-adolescent relations (Almeida and Galambos, 1991). Indeed, Crouter and Crowley (1990) found that fathers in dual-earner families spent similar amounts of time alone with their school-age daughters and sons, whereas fathers in single-earner families spent more time with sons. This may help explain the lack of differences between fathers' relations with their daughters and sons in the present sample of dual-earner families.

The present study contributes to our understanding of father-adolescent relations by documenting that relations between fathers and adolescents are continually evolving. Future research would further benefit our understanding by incorporating multiple age-related transitions into longitudinal studies in order to examine possible mechanisms underlying change in relationships (such as entrance into a particular peer group or school transitions). In addition, personal characteristics that fathers and adolescents bring to their relationship (for example, psychological well-being and temperamental characteristics) may contribute to changes in their relationship. By examining changes in father-adolescent relations and factors associated with such change, we can hope to better understand the vital role of father-adolescent relations in the lives of fathers and adolescents.

References

Alessandri, S. M., and Wozniak, R. H. "The Child's Awareness of Parental Beliefs Concerning the Child: A Developmental Study." Child Development, 1987, 58 (2), 316–323.

Alessandri, S. M., and Wozniak, R. H. "Continuity and Change in Intrafamilial Agreement in Beliefs Concerning the Adolescent: A Follow-up Study." Child Development, 1989, 60 (2), 335–339.

Almeida, D. M., and Galambos, N. L. "Examining Father Involvement and the Quality of Father-Adolescent Relations." Journal of Research on Adolescence, 1991, 1 (2), 155–172.

Armentrout, J., and Burger, G. "Children's Reports of Parental Childrearing Behavior at Five Grade Levels." Developmental Psychology, 1972, 7, 44–48.

Bird, G. W., Bird, G. A., and Scruggs, M. "Determinants of Family Task Sharing: A Study of Husbands and Wives." Journal of Marriage and the Family, 1984, 46 (2), 345–355.

Clark-Lempers, D. S., Lempers, J. D., and Ho, C. "Early, Middle, and Late Adolescents' Perceptions of Their Relationships with Significant Others." Journal of Adolescent Research, 1991, 6 (3), 296–315.

Collins, W. A., and Russell, G. "Mother-Child and Father-Child Relationships in Middle Childhood and Adolescence: A Developmental Analysis." Developmental Review, 1991, 11 (2), 99–136.

Crouter, A. C., and Crowley, M. S. "School-aged Children's Time Alone with Fathers in Dual- and Single-Earner Families: Implications for the Father-Adolescent Relationship." Journal of Early Adolescence, 1990, 10 (3), 296–312.

Crouter, A. C., Perry-Jenkins, M., Huston, T. L., and McHale, S. M. "Processes Underlying Father Involvement in Dual and Single Career Families." Developmental Psychology, 1987, 23 (3), 431–440.

Csikszentmihalyi, M., and Larson, R. Being Adolescent: Conflict and Growth in the Teenage Years. New York: Basic Books, 1984.

DeLuccie, M. F., and Davis, A. J. "Father-Child Relationships from the Preschool Years Through Mid-Adolescence." Journal of Genetic Psychology, 1991, 153 (2), 225–238.

Galambos, N. L., and Almeida, D. M. "Does Parent-Adolescent Conflict Increase During Early Adolescence?" Journal of Marriage and the Family, 1992, 54 (3), 737–747.

Galambos, N. L., and Maggs, J. L. "Out-of-School Care of Young Adolescents and Self-Reported Behavior." Developmental Psychology, 1991, 27 (4), 644–655.

Grotevant, H. D., and Cooper, C. R. "Patterns of Interaction in Family Relationships and the Development of Identity Exploration in Adolescence. Special Issue: Family Development." Child Development, 1985, 56 (2), 415–428.

Hill, J. P. "Research on Adolescents and Their Families: Past and Prospect." In C.E. Irwin, Jr. (ed.), Adolescent Social Behavior and Health. New Directions for Child Development, no. 37. San Francisco: Jossey-Bass, 1987.

Hill, J. P., Holmbeck, G. N., Marlow, L., Green, T., and Lynch, M. "Menarcheal Status and Parent-Child Relations in Families of Seventh-Grade Girls." Journal of Youth and Adolescence, 1985a, 14 (4), 301–316.

Hill, J. P., Holmbeck, G. N., Marlow, L., Green, T., and Lynch, M. "Pubertal Status and Parent-Child Relations in Families of Seventh-Grade Boys." Journal of Early Adolescence, 1985b, 5 (1), 31–44.

Little, R.J.A., and Rubin, O. B. Statistical Analysis with Missing Data. New York: Wiley, 1987.

Maccoby, E. E. Social Development: Psychological Growth and the Parent-Child Relationship. Orlando, Fla.: Harcourt Brace Jovanovich, 1980.

Maccoby, E. E. "Socialization and Developmental Change." Child Development, 1984, 55 (2), 317–328.

McNally, S., Eisenberg, N., and Harris, J. D. "Consistency and Change in Maternal Child-rearing Practices and Values: A Longitudinal Study." Child Development, 1991, 62 (1), 190–198.

Montemayor, R. "Parents and Adolescents in Conflict: All Families Some of the Time and Some Families Most of the Time." Journal of Early Adolescence, 1983, 3 (1), 83–103.

Montemayor, R., and Brownlee, J. R. "Fathers, Mothers, and Adolescents: Gender-based Differences in Parental Roles During Adolescence." Journal of Youth and Adolescence, 1987, 16 (3), 281–291.

Pleck, J. H. Working Wives/Working Husbands. Newbury Park, Calif.: Sage, 1985.

Prinz, R., Foster, S., Kent, R., and O'Leary, K. "Multivariate Assessment of Conflict in Distressed and Non-distressed Mother-Adolescent Dyads." Journal of Applied Behavioral Analysis, 1979, 12 (4), 691–700.

Roberts, G. C., Block, J. H., and Block, J. "Continuity and Change in Parents' Child-rearing Practices." Child Development, 1984, 55 (2), 586–597.

Schaefer, E. "Children's Reports of Parental Behavior: An Inventory." Child Development, 1965, 36, 417–424.

Smetana, J. G. "Adolescents' and Parents' Reasoning About Actual Family Conflict." Child Development, 1989, 60 (5), 1052–1067.

Steinberg, L. "Impact of Puberty on Family Relations: Effects of Pubertal Status and Pubertal Timing." Developmental Psychology, 1987, 23 (3), 451–460.

Steinberg, L. "Reciprocal Relation Between Parent-Child Distance and Pubertal Maturation." Developmental Psychology, 1989, 24 (1), 122–128.

Steinberg, L. "Autonomy, Conflict, and Harmony in the Family Relationship." In S. S. Feldman and G. R. Elliot (eds.), At the Threshold: The Developing Adolescent. Cambridge, Mass.: Harvard University Press, 1990.

Steinberg, L., and Hill, J. P. "Patterns of Family Interaction as a Function of Age, the Onset of Puberty, and Formal Thinking." Developmental Psychology, 1978, 14 (6), 683–684.

Wilkinson, L. SYSTAT: The System for Statistics. Evanston, Ill.: SYSTAT, 1988.

DAVID M. ALMEIDA is at the Institute for Social Research, University of Michigan, Ann Arbor.

NANCY L. GALAMBOS is associate professor at the Department of Psychology, University of Victoria, B.C., Canada.

Results of an exploration of the distinctive nature of father-adolescent relationships suggest that relationships with fathers are better models for a balanced closeness and separateness than relationships with mothers.

Distinctive Role of the Father in Adolescent Separation-Individuation

Shmuel Shulman, Moshe M. Klein

Research on parent-child interaction has shown consistent differences in fathers' and mothers' involvement with infants and young children. More recent studies on older children and adolescents have pointed to similar trends. The purpose of this chapter is to further explore the role of fathers and mothers during adolescence, to learn to what extent fathers' and mothers' roles are similar, and to identify the possible distinctive features of fathers' role during this stage of development. The basic contention, which is supported by the findings, is that fathers, by not being too involved and by showing respect for adolescent strivings for independence, serve as an adequate model and facilitate the separation-individuation process in adolescence.

Studies have shown that fathers spend less time with their preschool-age children than mothers (Lamb, 1987). For children in adolescence the findings are similar. Fathers are reported to spend one-third (Russell, 1983) or one-half (Montemayor and Brownlee, 1987) the amount of time that mothers do with their children. Adolescents, moreover, are more engaged in certain activities with mothers than with fathers (Montemayor and Brownlee, 1987). A greater proportion of time spent with fathers is in leisure or play. Similar trends in early childhood show that fathers are more playful with their infants, whereas mothers are more engaged in caregiving activities (Belsky, 1979).

However, other studies on younger children have shown a similar degree of involvement between mothers and fathers in cognitive and achievement-oriented interactions (Russell and Russell, 1987). Mothers and fathers were also found to be similarly involved in their children's school-related activities (Roberts, Block, and Block, 1984). We may then speculate that in some

New Directions for Child Development, no. 62, Winter 1993 © Jossey-Bass Publishers

contexts fathers are involved with their adolescents on at least a similar level as mothers.

Moreover, due to their traditional role, males have more interaction with the extrafamily environment (Parsons and Bales, 1955). Thus fathers may serve as models and promoters of their offspring's transactions outside of the family. Therefore it is possible that the lower involvement of fathers in the daily matters of their adolescents does not exclude interest in other areas, such as long-term achievement-related issues, professional identity, and relationships with the extrafamily environment.

Adolescents spend longer periods of time away from parents than younger children (Larson and Richards, 1991) and are less dependent on parents' care-giving. Thus it is reasonable to assume that parent-adolescent interactions occur in different contexts and cover different topics compared with parents' interactions with children of earlier ages. The fathers' level of involvement with their adolescents might be comparable to that of mothers, especially in domains related to achievement or extrafamily activities.

However, the fact that other studies have revealed that fathers are less engaged with their adolescent offspring than mothers cannot be dismissed. The question can be raised regarding the reason for this difference and its possible function. The difference between mothers' and fathers' involvement with their children has in the past been attributed mainly to historical and sociological causes. The male's role in society has been that of "soldier" with the primary function of protecting and providing (Mackey, 1985); he was the traditional breadwinner (Parsons and Bales, 1955). Male careers, particularly in the years when children are young, often require intense dedication and continual participation, and this undoubtedly interferes with father-child interactions (Stockard and Johnson, 1979). The last two decades have witnessed a growing number of women in the workforce, and women have become important or equal breadwinners. However, the level of fathers' involvement with their children remains low compared with that of mothers. In a Swedish sample of families in which the mother was employed, the paternal level of involvement was not significantly higher than in families where the mother was not employed (Lamb and others, 1988).

The lower level of paternal engagement combined with the findings that fathers are engaged in different types of interaction with their children, such as play and leisure activities, suggest that fathers' relationships are of a different nature from mothers'. In our discussion of relationships we have dealt with constructs that emphasize closeness and attachment. Kohut (1977) proposed the existence of two parallel lines in development; the first line is the well-known strand of attachment, and the second points to the need to develop an aspect of oneself separate from others. Similarly, Gilligan (1982) described two contrasting ways of relating to others. The first, essentially expressed by women, focuses on connectedness and closeness; the second, essentially expressed by men, focuses on separateness and differentiation. Grossman

(1987) found that more autonomous first-time fathers were doing better with their children. For adult men the ease of being separate contributed to their performance as fathers. Thus acting in a seemingly "disengaged" mode need not exclude interest and concern for the other; rather, it may reflect an additional mode of relatedness expressed mainly by men.

The penchant for separateness within the balance between closeness and separateness in close relationships does not characterize only fathers. Adolescents struggle with this issue in a similar manner. Approaching adolescence, children are more at ease by themselves and spend longer periods of time away from their parents. Not only do adolescents spend longer periods of time with peers, but even when at home they tend to be in their rooms, separate from their parents (Larson and Richards, 1991). When together, adolescents and parents tend to interrupt each other with increasing frequency, and growing deference is evidenced (Steinberg, 1981).

In addition, adolescents "separate" from the childish perceptions they have held of their parents. They stop idealizing their parents and tend to perceive them as ordinary people (Steinberg and Silverberg, 1986). Furthermore, whereas younger children tend to adhere to and respect parental authority (Smetana, 1989), adolescents tend to question or reject parental authority. Similar findings are expressed by psychoanalytic writers. Anna Freud (1958) described the need of the adolescent to withdraw the libido from parents so as not to feel too close to them. Blos (1967) emphasized the adolescent's need to relinquish dependencies on parents. Separateness from parents is evidenced both in increased physical separation and in a growing change in the relationship with parents that allows more room for adolescent autonomy.

The father who puts a stronger emphasis on separateness within a relationship and allows for more individuality may therefore be an appropriate model at the stage of adolescence. Less engagement by fathers with their offspring allows more room for the adolescent to express and exert individuality and to be responsible for his or her own actions. An important aspect of independence is the question of who makes the decision about a certain activity (Holmbeck, 1992). Collins and Luebker (1991) talk about the transfer of responsibilities to the adolescent. The lower involvement that may seem like paternal indifference and aloofness may serve as an incentive for the adolescent to attain individuality and responsibility. The fact that adolescents have been found to have less conflictful relationships with their fathers than with their mothers (Steinberg, 1987; Vuchinich, 1987) suggests that fathers may interfere less and respect more the independent behavior of their adolescents. Adolescents may therefore feel less need to oppose their fathers and feel more free to pursue their own interests.

However, it would be too simple to claim that fathers contribute to adolescent striving for separation and autonomy only by default, by not being too involved. Fathers have been found to show high respect for their offspring's individuality. For example, fathers who comment on and refer to their adolescent offspring's suggestions (even by showing disagreement) tend to have sons and daughters who reveal a higher level of identity exploration (Grotevant and Cooper, 1985). Moreover, fathers are found to use more enabling speech when interacting with their adolescents compared with mothers (Hauser and others, 1987). Thus, fathers more than mothers tend to support independent behaviors and expressions of their adolescents.

In addition to increased separation from parents and regulation of one's daily activities, positive emotions about one's own competence are a manifestation of autonomy. Blatt and Blass (1990) point to positive feelings such as self-esteem and self-confidence. Positive internalized feelings about oneself allow an individual to maintain a positive and active orientation in accomplishing goals. Berkowitz, Shapiro, Zinner, and Shapiro (1974) have suggested that when parents support their adolescent and show confidence in his or her choices, the adolescent's sense of self-esteem is validated and consolidated. The majority of relationship constructs, such as time together, communication, and closeness, exemplify mainly quantitative features (Collins and Repinski, in press). Fathers rated lower on these features than mothers; they appear to be less involved, exhibit less affect, and are less intimate toward their adolescents. However, the attainment of self-validation, reflected by such qualities as the reduction of fear about oneself, and learning about oneself and one's unique characteristics via an intimate disclosure, does not have to be related to the quantitative aspects of an interaction. LeCroy (1988) found that though fathers were less intimate with their adolescents, the level of intimacy with the father was a better predictor of adolescent adjustment than the level of intimacy with the mother.

In sum, our speculation is that fathers, as compared with mothers, express more support for adolescent autonomy and less expectation that their offspring will remain dependent on them. Moreover, because fathers' own inner models reflect separateness and personal space within a close relationship, their interaction with their adolescents, regardless of its magnitude, will be related to higher levels of adolescent autonomy. To explore these contentions, adolescents were interviewed regarding their joint activities with both parents, the availability of parents, and the extent to which each parent perceives the adolescent as still dependent or conveys the message that the adolescent can be relied on. The major purposes of the interview were to examine the nature and distinctiveness of interaction with each parent and to identify possible joint activities with parents that may support adolescent independence. The question was, to what extent are paternal and maternal interactions with the adolescent related to the adolescent's level of independence?

Relationships between parents and children during adolescence undergo changes following pubertal development (Steinberg, 1981); differences also occur in behavioral expectations of parents by children and vice versa (Collins, 1990). Thus an additional question was, do fathers and mothers adapt their attitudes toward their adolescents in line with the pace of development? Do fathers adapt their attitudes at a different pace than mothers? To answer this question, father-adolescent and mother-adolescent relationships were evaluated and compared across three age groups: twelve-year-olds (early adolescents), fourteen-year-olds (middle adolescents), and sixteen-year-olds (those in the later stages of adolescence).

Method

Subjects. Seventh, ninth, and eleventh graders residing in the Tel Aviv metro area were contacted at school and asked if they would participate in a study on parent-child relationships. Students whose parents gave written consent were included in the study. Seventy-eight adolescents participated, representing 89 percent of the students who were contacted. The distribution of subjects was as follows: twenty-eight seventh graders (eighteen males and ten females), mean age 12.4 years; twenty-nine ninth graders (thirteen males and sixteen females), mean age 14.6 years; and twenty-one eleventh graders (eight males and thirteen females), mean age 16.5 years.

The families were all intact and were predominantly middle-class. Fathers' mean age was 45.6 years (range 37–60), and 55 percent of them had college education. Mothers' mean age was 42.1 years (range 32–56), and 45 percent had college education.

Instruments and Procedures. Each adolescent was individually interviewed for about ninety minutes. The adolescents were asked to describe the activities they had been involved in with each parent in the prior week. In addition, adolescents were asked to rate (on a 1-to-5 scale) their perceptions in response to the following questions: (1) To what extent do you discuss the following topics with your father or mother: politics, studies, friends, sex, personal problems, family matters, and going out? (2) To what extent is your father or mother involved and an active participant in the following daily matters: how to dress, neatness, studies, what to eat, discipline, friends, and going out? (3) To what extent does your father or mother listen to and respect your ideas and wishes in the following domains: politics, what to study, what to do in the future, friends, sex, going out, how to dress, family matters, and problems that bother you?

The adolescents were also interviewed about the following areas: When does each parent come home from work? To what extent is each parent available to you? Would you like to spend more time with father or mother? What difference will it make? Is there something you do not do with your father or mother that you would like to do? Would you like father or mother to be more involved with you?

In addition, adolescents were asked to rate (on a 1-to-5 scale) the extent to which the father or mother conveys the feeling that the adolescent can be relied on to act independently, and the extent to which the father or mother behaves and acts as if the adolescent is still dependent on the parent. Finally, the adolescents were asked to describe their view of a good father and a good mother. What is the difference between a good father and a good mother?

The adolescents' reponses were transcribed and evaluated by two raters. Internal consistencies (Cronbach alphas) for adolescents' ratings on the various domains were as follows: frequency of discussions with parents, .81; parents' involvement, .76; and parental respect, .80.

Agreement between raters on topics such as parental availability, the youth's wish to spend more time with parents, and parents' perception of the adolescent as independent (can be relied on) or dependent, ranged from .84 to .91. Content analysis of activities in which adolescents are involved with parents yielded five main areas: playful activities at home such as computer games; outdoor playful activities such as going to a soccer game; caregiving; outdoor nonplayful activities such as shopping; and discussions with parents. Agreement between raters on classification of activities was .96.

The scores derived from the interviews reflect two constructs. The first construct represents the nature of interactions with each parent—type, frequency, parental availability, and parental respect for the adolescent. The second construct represents the extent to which parents perceive their adolescent as independent or dependent.

Results

Results will be presented and discussed along the following lines: (1) description and frequency of adolescents' interactions with fathers and mothers; (2) level of perceived parental involvement and availability, and adolescents' expectations for additional interaction with parents; (3) perceptions of parental respect for the adolescent's ideas and wishes, and support for adolescent independence; and (4) association between the nature and level of interaction with fathers and that with mothers, and parents' perception of the adolescent as independent or dependent.

Findings regarding age group and gender differences in father-adolescent and mother-adolescent interactions will be incorporated in the presentation of the results.

Frequency and Type of Interaction with Fathers and Mothers. Fathers, compared with mothers, were described as spending less time with their adolescents. Fathers returned home at around six o'clock in the evening (mean = 6.31, SD = 1.59). Twenty percent of mothers in the sample were homemakers. Those who work returned home around three o'clock in the afternoon (mean = 2.96; SD = 1.34) ($F = 107.49$ [$df = 1.47$], $p < .0001$).

The different types of activities in which fathers and mothers were described as engaged in with their adolescents are listed in Table 3.1. Fathers were more engaged in playful outdoor activities. Mothers spent more time at home in caregiving activities, especially with their younger adolescents. Mothers were more involved in outdoor nonplayful activities than fathers and more

Table 3.1. Weekly Frequencies of Types of Activities Fathers and Mothers Engage in with Their Twelve-, Fourteen-, and Sixteen-Year-Olds: Means, Standard Deviations (in Parentheses), and Significance of Differences

	Fathers			Mothers			Differences		
	Twelve-Year-Olds	Fourteen-Year-Olds	Sixteen-Year-Olds	Twelve-Year-Olds	Fourteen-Year-Olds	Sixteen-Year-Olds	Between Parents	Parent × Age	Parent × Sex
Playful activities at home	0.68 (0.77)	0.34 (0.48)	0.48 (0.60)	0.28 (0.53)	0.27 (0.52)	0.38 (0.58)	5.43*	—	5.92*
Outdoor playful activities	0.53 (0.79)	0.65 (0.89)	0.47 (0.75)	0.07 (0.26)	0.03 (0.18)	0.09 (0.30)	20.02**	—	—
Caregiving (home)	0.57 (0.83)	0.58 (0.73)	0.47 (0.75)	1.07 (0.76)	0.48 (0.69)	0.76 (0.70)	—	3.50*	—
Outdoor nonplayful activities (shopping)	0.64 (0.91)	0.44 (0.68)	0.33 (0.66)	0.85 (1.04)	0.86 (0.74)	0.76 (0.90)	8.18***	—	4.63*
Discussions	0.03 (0.19)	0.31 (0.66)	0.19 (0.40)	0.28 (0.46)	0.41 (0.50)	0.61 (0.49)	13.33**	—	4.43*

Note: Playful activities were performed more by fathers with boys; outdoor nonplayful activities and discussions were performed more by mothers with girls.

*p < .05
**p < .01
***p < .001

with their daughters. A similar trend was found regarding parent-adolescent discussions: mothers had more discussions with their adolescents, especially their adolescent daughters.

More specifically, regarding discussions with fathers and mothers, mothers were described as engaged in discussions with their adolescents across topics and ages more than fathers. Mothers were described as more involved in discussing personal problems and family matters as well as issues related to adolescents' peers. The one exception was that fathers tended to discuss politics with their adolescents more than mothers did (F = 16.07 [df = 1.70], p < .001). The majority of differences between mothers and fathers were consistent across age and gender.

Level of Parental Involvement and Availability. Generally, results showed that mothers, compared with fathers, were more involved with their adolescents in daily matters, such as what to wear, what to eat, and when and with whom to socialize (see Table 3.2). Yet for "nonmundane" issues such as studies or discipline, fathers' level of involvement was no different from that of mothers.

The higher level of maternal daily involvement was also reflected in adolescents' ratings of parental availability. Mothers were perceived to be more available (mean = 4.51, SD = 0.68) than fathers (mean = 4.14, SD = 0.82) (F = 13.93 [df = 1.70], p < .001). Here, too, differences between fathers' and mothers' perceived involvement and availability were generally found across adolescent age and gender.

Regarding adolescents' expectations for additional interactions with parents, on the whole, they reported that they feel they spend enough time with their parents. When asked what else they would like to do with their parents, clear differences regarding mothers and fathers emerged. Boys did not wish to spend more time with their mothers. Boys, especially the twelve-year-olds, clearly expressed the wish to be more involved with their fathers in outdoor activities (^{2} = 4.66, p < .05). At younger ages (twelve and fourteen) the majority of girls expressed no wish to be more engaged with either parent. Yet almost half of the sixteen-year-old girls expressed their wish to be more engaged with both parents.

All in all, results showed that fathers, compared with mothers, spent less time with their adolescents and were less involved in their day-to-day issues. However, with crucial issues such as studies at stake, fathers' level of involvement was not different from that of mothers. When together with their adolescents, fathers tended to be more involved in playful and outdoor activities.

Parental Respect and Support for Adolescent Independence. When asked whether parents listen to and respect their ideas in personal, family, and general matters, adolescents on the whole reported that they were well respected by both parents (more than 4 on a scale of 1 to 5). Yet when adolescents were asked specifically whether parents foster dependence or whether parents rely on them to be independent, a clear difference between fathers and mothers emerged (see Table 3.3). Compared with mothers, fathers were

Table 3.2. Levels of Father and Mother Involvement in Seven Daily Matters Across Three Age Levels: Means, Standard Deviations (in Parentheses), and Significance of Differences

	Fathers			Mothers			Differences		
	Twelve-Year-Olds	Fourteen-Year-Olds	Sixteen-Year-Olds	Twelve-Year-Olds	Fourteen-Year-Olds	Sixteen-Year-Olds	Between Parents	Parent Age	Parent Sex
What to wear	3.10 (1.37)	2.92 (1.07)	2.47 (1.20)	4.32 (0.90)	4.14 (1.02)	3.95 (1.02)	10.29*	—	—
Appearance[a]	3.78 (0.78)	3.44 (1.01)	3.19 (1.43)	4.50 (0.74)	4.48 (0.75)	3.95 (1.20)	35.97**	—	—
Studies	4.39 (0.87)	4.25 (0.94)	4.00 (1.22)	4.64 (0.56)	4.29 (0.86)	4.19 (1.24)	—	—	—
Eating habits	3.46 (1.26)	3.59 (1.00)	3.14 (1.27)	4.32 (0.98)	4.40 (0.69)	4.14 (0.79)	54.50*	—	—
Discipline[a]	3.96 (0.89)	4.03 (1.05)	3.42 (1.32)	4.22 (0.84)	3.96 (0.93)	3.43 (1.32)	—	3.39***	—
Friends[b]	3.25 (1.17)	3.22 (1.12)	2.90 (1.04)	4.00 (1.08)	4.03 (0.85)	3.85 (1.23)	45.83*	—	—
Going out	3.60 (1.22)	3.40 (1.27)	2.95 (1.32)	4.07 (0.89)	3.77 (1.08)	3.57 (1.39)	16.98*	—	—

[a] Significant age differences were found.

[b] Parents are more involved with daughters.

*p < .001

**p < .01

***p < .05

Table 3.3. Level of Parental Emphasis on Adolescent Dependence or Reliance Across Three Age Levels: Means, Standard Deviations (in Parentheses), and Significance of Differences

	Fathers			Mothers			Differences		
	Twelve-Year-Olds	Fourteen-Year-Olds	Sixteen-Year-Olds	Twelve-Year-Olds	Fourteen-Year-Olds	Sixteen-Year-Olds	Between Parents	Parent Age	Parent Sex
Views you as being dependent[a]	3.40 (1.08)	2.77 (0.89)	2.47 (0.98)	3.70 (0.79)	3.59 (0.69)	3.28 (0.84)	65.95*	3.65**	—
Relies on you	4.35 (0.73)	4.48 (0.75)	4.28 (1.05)	3.89 (0.87)	3.59 (0.63)	3.95 (0.80)	34.55*	—	—

[a] Significant age differences were found.

*$p < .001$

**$p < .05$

described as perceiving their adolescents as less dependent. In addition, the older the youngsters, the less the father was reported to perceive the adolescent as dependent. Across all three age groups fathers were perceived to convey to their adolescents the sense that they can be relied on. Mothers, on the other hand, regardless of age group, were reported to perceive the adolescent as more dependent and to rely on them less compared with fathers.

Further distinctions in the role of fathers were revealed by adolescents' responses to the open questions: What is a good father? What is a good mother? Content analysis of these data showed that, on the whole, perceptions of the "good father" and of the "good mother" are quite similar. Almost all adolescents emphasized that a good parent, either father or mother, is involved, loves, helps, does things for the child, and engages in discussions.

Yet further probing revealed some distinctions between the roles of father and mother, as illustrated in the following vignettes:

"A father is more preoccupied by work, a mother has more free time for her children and therefore they turn to her. A mother loves her child as a father does but she really does it. A father is more like a friend with whom you do things together" (male, age twelve).

"A good mother is more at home, which is impossible for a good father because he works" (female, age twelve).

"A good mother is more at home and therefore she is more aware of what's going on. A good father is less at home, cannot be aware of everything that happens and what he does see, sees from a different perspective" (female, age twelve).

"A good mother pampers more, helps me, teaches me to cook. A good father helps mainly in learning new things, building things" (male, age fourteen).

"A good father is more strict and more peerlike; a good mother cares, more at home" (male, age twelve).

The majority of the adolescents, across age and gender, drew the traditional distinctions between the roles of father and mother, emphasizing that fathers, due to their obligations at work, spend less time with them. However, during the times when fathers are at home, they were described as introducing additional perspectives into the relationship. Fathers were described as combining "parental" and "peerlike" roles in their interactions with their adolescents.

Interactions with Parents and Adolescent Independence. Correlations between level of perceived parental reliance on adolescent independence and interactions with both fathers and mothers further highlighted the distinctive role of fathers. As shown in Table 3.4, paternal involvement with the adolescents, whether caring for the youngster or discussing things with him or her, was positively related to paternal level of reliance. Fathers' involvement with their adolescents did not interfere with their support of adolescent independence. On the contrary, through their involvement fathers even supported ado-

Table 3.4. Correlations Between Level of Paternal and Maternal Reliance on Adolescent and Measures of Interactions with Father or Mother (N = 76)

	Views as Being Dependent	General Level of Involvement	General Frequency of Discussions	General Respect
Father	.22*	.28**	.45***	.41***
Mother	−.04	.02	.09	.42***

$*p < .05$

$**p < .01$

$***p < .001$

lescent individuation. Maternal involvement, however, was not related to the tendency of mothers to rely on their adolescent. Through their involvement mothers apparently did not convey the sense that they rely on their adolescents to be independent. Only clear maternal respect for the adolescent's views was found to be related to a sense of being relied on.

Discussion

The results from the study showed that fathers spent less time with their adolescents, were less involved with them, and spent a lower amount of time discussing personal and family matters. These findings are similar to those reported on U.S. middle-class samples (Collins and Russell 1991; Montemayor and Brownlee, 1987; Steinberg, 1987). However, fathers were not considered absent by their adolescents. Adolescents described their fathers as breadwinners, and they understood and accepted the lesser amount of time spent with them. Moreover, for important matters such as studies or discipline, fathers were not described as less involved than mothers. Goodnow and Collins (1990) reported that when crucial issues, such as inappropriate behavior of the child, are at stake, fathers can be as involved as mothers.

Adolescents were probably aware that fathers can be available in time of need, though fathers were less continuously present. When asked to describe the difference between a good father and a good mother, a fourteen-year-old adolescent replied, "During adolescence the father is more important than the mother. New concerns like school, friends, and 'boys' issues' arise. Fathers know better how to deal with such issues. Matters that the mother was responsible for like what to eat or taking a bath become less important as you grow up." The findings and the reflection by this fourteen-year-old suggest that during adolescence the immediate presence of the parent is less crucial. What counts more is the child's confidence in the availability of the parent. Attachment theories emphasize that secure attachment is based on the confidence in the caregiver's availability, and not on the person's immediate and continuous presence (Ainsworth, Blehar, Waters, and Wall, 1987).

Knowing that a close person is available makes it easier to stay for some time by oneself, and solitude may then have positive aspects. Larson (1990) found that adolescents who spend some time by themselves were better adjusted. The limited time with the father may therefore have a similar positive impact, signaling to the adolescent that he or she can be more responsible.

Findings of the current study also showed that, when together, fathers and adolescents were more engaged in playful and outdoor activities. Play is an activity that is flexible, pleasant, and not aimed at some end (Smith and Volstedt, 1985). During play, relationships between fathers and adolescents are probably quite egalitarian, as expected between players. Experiencing an egalitarian relationship lowers the sense of dependence and increases one's feelings of competence. Thus fathers' relationships with their adolescents recall to some extent peerlike relationships (Youniss and Smollar, 1985). Peers are less critical of each other and more respectful of each other's views, and such relationships may promote independence. These findings suggest that father-adolescent relationships do not have to be evaluated only from a quantitative perspective.

Findings also showed that, although they spend less time together, adolescents perceived fathers' attitudes as supporting adolescent striving for growth. Mothers, as portrayed by adolescents, tended to grant less autonomy to their offspring and were less likely to rely on them as independent individuals. As mentioned earlier, an important facet of autonomy is positive emotions about one's own competence (Blatt and Blass, 1990). Fathers, more than mothers, conveyed the feeling that they can rely on their adolescents; thus fathers might serve as a "facilitating environment" (Shulman and Klein, 1982, p. 223) for adolescent attainment of differentiation from the family and consolidation of independence.

The current study did not deal explicitly with the ways in which fathers lead or guide their adolescents to independence. It was suggested that, by their lower level of involvement and peerlike relationships, fathers indirectly support adolescent individuation. Other studies have suggested that fathers may also use more directive ways to guide their offspring to independence. Hauser and others (1987) interviewed fathers and mothers of adolescents regarding the behaviors that they were encouraging and discouraging. Parents were also asked what do they do to encourage or discourage a certain behavior. Results showed that fathers saw themselves as more actively involved than mothers in encouraging instrumental behaviors such as assertiveness and independence. However, fathers tended more than mothers to punish their adolescents while encouraging independence. A similar phenomenon is found among Mexican fathers. Whereas Mexican fathers are affectionate with younger children, they become distant as children enter puberty. Fathers then become stern and employ discipline to transmit societal values in order to turn the adolescent into a grown-up member of society (Madsen, 1973). The combination of flexible and strict approaches by fathers in relating to their adolescents was also reflected by a twelve-year-old boy asked to compare a good father and a good mother: "A good father is more strict and more peerlike; a good mother cares, more at home."

The understanding of ways fathers employ to foster independence deserves further attention and research. However, it is clear from our results that fathers are at ease both being close and being separate. Fathers' involvement with their adolescents was related to their support of adolescent independence. The father's involvement with the adolescent did not lead to interference with his or her need for independence, but rather supported it. These results are in line with our contention that men and women have different models of close relationships. Men are more capable of emphasizing separateness within a close relationship (Gilligan, 1982; Grossman, 1989). Though fathers are perceived as more distant by their growing adolescents (Shulman, Collins, and Dital, 1993), adolescents do not feel that their fathers are absent and they emphasize fathers' support for independence. Mothers are perceived by their adolescents as closer but are also more perceived as fostering dependence.

Recent studies and theories have focused on the different aspects of separation-individuation. Whereas one approach emphasizes the importance of emotional disengagement, another underscores the evolving mutuality in a more differentiated parent-adolescent relationship (Frank and Burke, 1992; Ryan and Lynch, 1989; Steinberg and Silverberg, 1986). The first approach recalls our findings on maternal attitudes toward adolescents, where independence must be separated from involvement. The other approach recalls our findings on fathers' attitudes. Separation-individuation is a dialectical process whereby adolescents increase the amount of distance between themselves and their parents in an attempt to gain in separateness and self-directedness yet avoid excessive estrangement by maintaining a sense of relatedness (Frank, Pirsch, and Wright, 1990). Being distant does not necessarily convey, as fathers show in their behavior and attitudes, being detached.

During adolescence parental perceptions of and behavior toward their children are expected to change to adapt to the maturational development of their offspring (Collins, 1990). Patterns of perceived parent-child relationships according to the three age groups twelve, fourteen, and sixteen were quite similar. The only exceptions were that sixteen-year-olds reported that both parents discuss fewer issues concerning peers, are less involved with their appearance, and use less discipline. Thus, in general and contrary to our expectations, fathers' and mothers' attitudes were not found to change with the age of their adolescents.

However, the results show that adolescents' dependence on fathers significantly decreased with age whereas dependence on mothers did not significantly change with age. Taken together, these results seem to indicate a tendency for fathers to be more distant from their adolescents, and this tendency does not change over time. However, as the adolescent becomes older, his or her perception is that dependency on the father decreases while dependency on the mother does not change. The father may then be perceived as the person who can support the adolescent's struggle to contain maternal engulfment (Blos, 1990).

In summary, we have described some distinctions between mothers' and fathers' roles in adolescence and suggested that fathers may be more appropriate models for separation-individuation. Yet a few conceptual and research questions require further investigation. First, it was argued that fathers' interactions with their adolescents should not be restricted to the quantitative aspects for which fathers were consistently found to be less engaged than mothers. Qualitative aspects of interactions should be operationalized and could be studied in terms of children's and parents' perceptions. An additional finding was that the father gives more support for adolescent independence and also serves as a model for balanced closeness and separateness. It would be interesting to investigate how this model is carried forward into adolescent behavior and functioning. Do fathers directly encourage adolescent individuation, and what ways do they employ? Do fathers actively guide and lead adolescents to assume more responsibility, or do fathers indirectly convey their messages for individuation by serving as models for adolescent development of positive attitudes toward individuation?

Results in the current study were based on interviews with adolescents. Interviews of parents as well as the employment of objective measures could further contribute to our understanding. In addition, generalizations should be made cautiously. This study was conducted on a sample of middle-class, intact families. Fathers may have a different role in a lower-class milieu or in single-parent families (Youniss and Ketterlinus, 1987). In a lower class, for example, fathers may be more disciplinary toward their adolescents (Bronstein, 1984). Further conceptualizations and studies using various measures of parent-child relationships may further contribute to the understanding of fathers' role in adolescent development.

References

Ainsworth, M.D.S., Blehar, M., Waters, E., and Wall, S. Patterns of Attachment. Hillsdale, N.J.: Erlbaum, 1978.

Belsky, J. "Mother-Father-Infant Interaction: A Naturalistic Observational Study." Developmental Psychology, 1979, 15, 601–607.

Berkowitz, D., Shapiro, R., Zinner, J., and Shapiro, E. "Family Contributions to Narcissistic Disturbances in Adolescence." International Review of Psychoanalysis, 1974, 1, 353–372.

Blatt, S. J., and Blass, R. B. "Attachment and Separateness: A Dialectical Model of the Products and Processes of Development Throughout the Life Cycle." Psychoanalytic Study of the Child, 1990, 45, 107–127.

Blos, P. "The Second Individuation Process of Adolescence." Psychoanalytic Study of the Child, 1967, 22, 162–186.

Blos, P. "Son and Father." In S. I. Greenspan and G. H. Pollack (eds.), The Course of Life, Vol. 4: Adolescence. Madison, Conn.: International Universities Press, 1990.

Bronstein, P. "Differences in Mothers' and Fathers' Behavior Toward Children: A Cross-Cultural Comparison." Developmental Psychology, 1984, 20, 995–1003.

Collins, W. A. "Parent-Child Relationships in the Transition to Adolescence: Continuity and Change in Interaction, Affect and Cognition." In R. Montemayor, G. R. Adams, and T. P. Gullota (eds.), From Childhood to Adolescence: A Transitional Period? Newbury Park, Calif.: Sage, 1990.

Collins, W. A., and Luebker, C. "Change in Parent-Child Relationships: Bilateral Processes in the Transition to Adolescence." Paper presented at the meetings of the International Society for the Study of Behavioral Development, Minneapolis, Minn. July 1991.

Collins, W. A., and Repinski, D. J. "Relationships During Adolescence: Continuity and Change in Interpersonal Perspective." In R. Montemayor, G. R. Adams, and T. P. Gullota (eds.), Advances in Adolescent Development, Vol. 5: Personal Relationships During Adolescence. Newbury Park, Calif.: Sage, in press.

Collins, W. A., and Russell, G. "Mother-Child and Father-Child Relationships in Middle Childhood and Adolescence: A Developmental Analysis." Developmental Review, 1991, 11, 99–136.

Frank, S. J., and Burke, L. "Deidealization and Autonomy in Late Adolescence: Replications and Extensions of Earlier Findings." Paper presented at the fourth biennial meeting of the Society for Research on Adolescence, Washington, D. C., March 1992.

Frank, S. J., Pirsch, L. A., and Wright, W. C. "Late Adolescents' Perceptions of Their Relationships with Their Parents: Relationships Among Deidealization, Autonomy, Relatedness, and Insecurity and Implications for Adolescent Adjustment and Ego Identity Status." Journal of Youth and Adolescence, 1990, 19, 571-588.

Freud, A. "Adolescence." Psychoanalytic Study of the Child, 1958, 13, 255–278.

Gilligan, C. In a Different Voice. Cambridge, Mass.: Harvard University Press, 1982.

Goodnow, J. J., and Collins, W. A. Development According to Parents: The Nature, Sources and Consequences of Parents' Ideas. Hove, England: Erlbaum, 1990.

Grossman, S. K. "Separate and Together: Men's Autonomy and Affiliation in the Transition to Parenthood." In P. W. Berman and F. A. Pedersen (eds.), Men's Transition to Parenthood. Hillsdale, N.J.: Erlbaum, 1989.

Grotevant, H. D., and Cooper, C. R. "Patterns of Interaction in Family Relationships and Development of Identity Exploration in Adolescence." Child Development, 1985, 56, 415–428.

Hauser, S. T., Book, B. K., Houlinahn, J., Powers, S., Weiss-Perry, B., Follansbee, D., Jacobson, A. M., and Noam, G. "Sex Differences Within the Family: Studies of Adolescent and Parent Family Interaction." Journal of Youth and Adolescence, 1987, 16, 199–213.

Holmbeck, G. N. "Autonomy and Psychosocial Adjustment in Adolescents with and Without Spina Bifida." Paper presented at the fourth biennial meeting of the Society for Research on Adolescence, Washington, D.C., March 1992.

Kohut, H. The Restoration of the Self. Madison, Conn.: International Universities Press, 1977.

Lamb, M. E. The Father's Role: Cross-Cultural Perspectives. New York: Wiley, 1987.

Lamb, M. E., Hwang, C. R., Bookstein, F. L., Bromberg, A., Hult, G., and Frodi, M. "Determinants of Social Competence in Swedish Preschoolers." Developmental Psychology, 1988, 24, 58–70.

Larson, R. W. "The Solitary Side of Life." Developmental Review, 1990, 10, 155–183.

Larson, R. W., and Richards, M. H. "Daily Companionship in Late Childhood and Early Adolescence: Changing Developmental Contexts." Child Development, 1991, 62, 284–300.

LeCroy, C. W. "Parent-Adolescent Intimacy: Impact on Adolescent Functioning." Adolescence, 1988, 23, 137–147.

Mackey, W. C. "A Cross-Cultural Perspective on Perceptions of Paternalistic Deficiencies in the US: The Myth of the Derelict Daddy." Sex Roles, 1985, 12, 509–533.

Madsen, W. The Mexican-American of South Texas. Troy, Mo.: Holt, Rinehart & Winston, 1973.

Montemayor, R., and Brownlee, J. R. "Fathers, Mothers and Adolescents: Gender-based Differences in Parental Roles During Adolescence." Journal of Youth and Adolescence, 1987, 16, 281–291.

Parsons, T. E., and Bales, R. F. Family Socialization and Interaction Processes. New York: Free Press, 1955.

Roberts, G., Block, J. H., and Block, J. "Continuity and Change in Parents' Child-rearing Practices." *Child Development,* 1984, *55,* 586–597.

Russell, G. *The Changing Role of Fathers.* Brisbane, Australia: University of Queensland Press, 1983.

Russell, G., and Russell, A. "Mother-Child and Father-Child Relationships in Middle Childhood." *Child Development,* 1987, *58,* 1573–1585.

Ryan, R. M., and Lynch, J. H. "Emotional Autonomy Versus Detachment: Revisiting the Vicissitudes of Adolescence and Young Adulthood." *Child Development,* 1989, *60,* 340–356.

Shulman, S., Collins, W. A., and Dital, M. "Parent-Child Relationships and Peer-Perceived Competence During Middle Childhood and Preadolescence in Israel." *Journal of Early Adolescence,* 1993, *13,* 204–218.

Shulman, S., and Klein, M. M. "The Family and Adolescence: A Conceptual and Experimental Approach." *Journal of Adolescence,* 1982, *5,* 219–234.

Smetana, J. G. "Adolescents' and Parents' Reasoning About Actual Family Conflict." *Child Development,* 1989, *60,* 1052–1067.

Smith, P. K., and Volstedt, R. "On Defining Play: An Empirical Study of the Relationship Between Play and Various Play Criteria." *Child Development,* 1985, *56,* 1042–1050.

Steinberg, L. "Transformations in Family Relations at Puberty." *Developmental Psychology,* 1981, *17,* 833–840.

Steinberg, L. "Impact of Puberty on Family Relations: Effects of Pubertal Status and Pubertal Timing." *Developmental Psychology,* 1987, *23,* 451–460.

Steinberg, L., and Silverberg, S. "The Vicissitudes of Autonomy in Early Adolescence." *Child Development,* 1986, *57,* 841–851.

Stockard, J., and Johnson, M. M. "The Social Origins of Male Dominance." *Sex Roles,* 1979, *5,* 199–218.

Vuchinich, S. "Starting and Stopping Spontaneous Family Conflicts." *Journal of Marriage and the Family,* 1987, *49,* 591–601.

Youniss, J., and Ketterlinus, R. D. "Communication and Connectedness in Mother- and Father-Adolescent Relationships." *Journal of Youth and Adolescence,* 1987, *16,* 265–280.

Youniss, J., and Smollar, S. *Adolescent Relations with Mothers, Fathers and Friends.* Chicago: Chicago University Press, 1985.

Shmuel Shulman is senior lecturer of clinical psychology in the Department of Psychology, Bar Ilan University, Ramat Gan, Israel. His main interests are adolescent development and family systems and therapy.

Moshe M. Klein is senior lecturer of clinical psychology in the Department of Psychology, Bar Ilan University, Ramat Gan, Israel. His main interest is family therapy.

Theory and research on male midlife development are reviewed. Data are presented that show a strong relationship between male midlife stress and the quality of father-adolescent communication.

Men in Midlife and the Quality of Father-Adolescent Communication

Raymond Montemayor, Patrick C. McKenry, Teresa Julian

In this chapter we examine male midlife development in the context of the father-adolescent relationship. We are specifically interested in father-adolescent communication. In contrast to most current literature on father-adolescent communication, which focuses on adolescents, we examine communication from the perspective of fathers.

We first review theory and research on the psychological development of men in midlife, focusing specifically on male midlife stress. Although not all fathers of adolescents are middle-aged, the majority have ages between the middle thirties and middle forties, a time when, for many men, certain midlife developmental themes emerge.

Next we examine the reciprocal influence of male midlife concerns and the father-adolescent relationship. In our view, development continues throughout adulthood, and the development of fathers both influences and is influenced by their relationships with their adolescent children. Theory and research on male midlife development are reviewed, and findings from an exploratory study are presented.

Male Midlife Stress

Traditionally, adulthood has been viewed as a period of psychological stability. Freud theorized that an individual's character structure is formed during early childhood, becomes fixed in late childhood, and remains unchanged throughout adulthood. In contrast to the importance Freud placed on early experience, most contemporary theorists interested in personality development suggest that personality develops throughout life.

NEW DIRECTIONS FOR CHILD DEVELOPMENT, no. 62, Winter 1993 © Jossey-Bass Publishers

Within the past few years there has been a growing interest in and awareness of one particular aspect of adult development, what has been termed
"midlife crisis." Until recently, most writing and research on this issue was
about women, primarily focusing on the impact of menopause on women's
behavior and on changes that occur to women when the last child moves out
of the house. It was assumed that women underwent dramatic changes during midlife when children move away from home, leading to the "empty-nest
syndrome" and to a decline in life satisfaction. Research on the empty nest
reveals that the majority of women do not experience a lasting crisis when their
children leave home, although some temporary decline in self-esteem and in
marital satisfaction may occur for some women, especially full-time homemakers (Borland, 1982). More recently, clinicians and researchers on adult
development have focused less on empty-nest issues and more on male midlife
transitions.

Several important clinical interview studies of adult development were
conducted in the mid 1970s, and the results were published as popular books
(Gould, 1978; Levinson, 1978; Sheehy, 1976; Vaillant, 1977). One theme to
emerge from these investigations was that midlife is a period of personality and
social transition for many men, one that sometimes leads to midlife stress. All
these studies were based on nonrandom samples and relied on qualitative data,
yet the finding that midlife is a stressful period for many men was widely
accepted in the popular press and led to attempts by social scientists to more
rigorously examine this idea.

A small but growing body of empirical research exists on male midlife
development, although limitations remain with research in this area. The primary problem is that a clear definition of male midlife transition has not yet
been formulated. Researchers define midlife stress in many ways and usually
do not distinguish it from other kinds of stress and from stress during other
periods of life. Distinctions are not drawn between midlife stress and crisis,
terms that are often used interchangeably. Because of these conceptual problems, a widely accepted and psychometrically strong midlife stress scale has
not been constructed.

In this chapter we are specifically interested in whether midlife is a transitional period for men and whether that period is stressful. We review literature in this area and draw generalizations where they seem appropriate. We do
not focus on sampling or methodological problems, but we do discuss these
problems as obstacles to generalizability.

Several explanations have been offered for why men in midlife may experience some disruption in their development that could lead to a crisis or at
least a temporary period of stress. From the time men reach their late thirties
there is a gradual decline in testosterone and cortisol levels and in the secretion of androgens (Brim, 1976). Little is known about the causes of these hor-
monal changes during midlife, their impact on self-concept and behavior, or
their possible contributions to midlife concerns. Brim (1976) contends that

these internal changes lead to external physical changes that make middle-aged men aware that they are aging. Brim and others argue that physical changes such as loss of hair, the need for reading glasses, decreased strength and stamina, and a decline in sexual interest and performance lead to a heightened awareness of one's own mortality. Further, men in their forties and fifties show the highest rates of stress-related illnesses, such as peptic ulcers, hypertension, and heart disease (see, for example, Lowenthal and Chiriboga, 1972). According to Neugarten (1968), these physical changes lead to a new attitude toward life, which she describes as a shift from "time-since-birth" to "time-left-to-live."

Besides midlife changes in physical condition and health, several important social transitions commonly occur in the lives of men in their forties and fifties. No aspect of a man's life is more central to his identity than his occupation, especially among middle-class, white-collar workers (Lowenthal, Thurnher, and Chiriboga, 1975). During midlife some men go through a career identity adjustment and experience this period as a time of unfulfilled dreams. Levinson (1978) uses the concept of "dream" to mean the aspirations and goals one sets for oneself in late adolescence. Based on interviews with the men in his study, Levinson reported that some middle-aged men come to the conclusion that they did not accomplish all they hoped for when they were younger and will never completely fulfill their earlier dreams. Besides changes in men's career aspirations, during this period children enter adolescence or leave home; wives begin working; and parents age, become more dependent, and eventually die.

The physical and social changes that are common in midlife are thought to be the catalysts for personality change. Based on clinical evidence and case studies, Levinson (1978) and Tamir (1982) suggest that something unique happens to men as they become middle-aged. At midlife some men reappraise and modify or relinquish many of the goals and values they formed during their own adolescent identity search. According to Tamir, this reappraisal necessitates unlearning old behaviors, learning new ways of engaging the world and people in it, and coming to terms with one's interior emotional life.

Variation exists in the occurrence, timing, and intensity of physical and social change. Further, men differ in their coping skills and social support, and all of this should result in variation in the level of midlife stress. For some men this period of life may be stressful and troublesome, and for others midlife may be a seamless continuation of earlier life. Vaillant (1977), among others, argues that many men reach their most stable and satisfying adaptation during this period of life. For example, in regard to occupations, middle-aged men hold the highest-status jobs and earn higher salaries than men of other ages (Borland, 1978). Farrell and Rosenberg (1981) report that only 12 percent of the men in their study experienced overt crisis during midlife, although more than half showed some evidence of stress and personal disorganization, and less than a third manifested a true sense of positive adaptation. Some researchers contend that midlife stress occurs only when change is unexpected and non-normative, as in the case of divorce, early death of a spouse, or job loss (Lowenthal, Thurnher, and Chiriboga, 1975; Neugarten, 1968). If we know little about the dimensions and qualities of male midlife stress, we know even less about individual variation in this transition.

Sex-Role Convergence Theory

Jung (1933) provides one framework for conceptualizing midlife transformation based on his theory of personality development. According to Jung, midlife is a period when new personality characteristics emerge after lying dormant since childhood. It is in the middle years that men begin to develop and express character traits such as nurturance, affiliation, and cooperation, which are traditionally considered "feminine." Jung claims that the socialization of males focuses on the formation of instrumental masculine qualities and on the repression of expressive feminine characteristics. Being independent, dominant, and competitive may be adaptive during early adulthood, when men establish themselves in their careers and provide for a family with small children. But as men grow older and move into the middle stages of their careers, as children enter adolescence and prepare to leave home, and as wives come to the end of child caretaking responsibilities, a continuing emphasis on the masculine side of personality and neglect of the feminine side may be unnecessary and even unhealthy. The idea that a man's identity enlarges during midlife to include traditionally female qualities is referred to as sex-role convergence theory (Moreland, 1980).

Another interpretation of the transition in sex roles during midlife is that many middle-aged men redefine masculinity for themselves to include qualities that before were excluded (Keen, 1991). From this modern perspective gender roles are socially constructed and modified with age. Men do not become more feminine or take on feminine qualities as they grow older, but instead expand their definition of masculinity to include qualities that at an earlier age were rejected because they were seen as feminine. These new qualities are incorporated into an already existing personality, modified, and expressed within that structure. For example, as men grow older they may become more nurturant, but that nurturance might be expressed by teaching and mentoring rather than through emotionally soothing talk.

Several researchers have shown that some degree of sex-role convergence occurs for many men during midlife (Gutmann, 1969; Lowenthal and Chiriboga, 1972; Neugarten, 1968; Tamir, 1982). Neugarten and Gutmann (1958) report that men at midlife become more nurturant, sensitive, and dependent and less aggressive. Lowenthal, Thurnher, and Chiriboga (1975) found that middle-aged working-class men reported increases in the values of dependency and nurturance and decreases in instrumental and material values.

Cross-cultural studies of adult development support the generality of sex-role convergence theory (Gutmann, 1969). Gutmann did field work on adult development among Mayan Indians in Mexico, Navajo Indians in Arizona, and the Galilean and Syrian Druze. He reported that in all these cultures, as men aged, risk taking declined and men became less competitive and more interested in protecting what they had already acquired. While men became more sensitive and loving and less aggressive, middle-aged women in these cultures became more competitive and assertive. Gutmann (1987) proposed that a gradual shift in personality organization normally occurs with the phasing out of parental duties. As children become more self-sufficient during adolescence, both parents can shift from traditional parenting roles, in which males provide and females nurture, to more androgynous behavior. During midlife, when responsibility to financially provide for their families decreases, men have an opportunity to express the emotional aspects of their personality.

Sex-role convergence during middle age, especially the development of emotional awareness and interest in relationships, has been shown to be positively related to the psychological well-being of men. Livson (1981) studied men in their fifties and reported that those men classified as psychologically "healthy" possessed positive opposite-sex qualities such as nurturance, whereas psychologically "unhealthy" men were high on negative feminine qualities such as dependence. In addition, the overall life satisfaction of these men was positively related to valuing emotional expressivity and interpersonal relationships.

Male sex-role convergence may be an adaptive response to a decrease in work orientation during middle age. Adherence to a traditional male role is seen by some as detrimental to the development of mutually satisfying interpersonal relations at all ages (Cohen, 1979; Pleck, 1981), but especially during middle age, when many men develop a deeper interest in fostering and maintaining relations with family members and friends. In regard to the marital relationship, for example, a traditional male role does not necessarily interfere with satisfactory husband-wife relations in midlife if the wife also is traditional, but it is related to lower marital quality when the wife has a modern, nontraditional sex-role orientation (Bowen and Orthner, 1983).

The finding that sex-role convergence among men in midlife is positively associated with measures of psychological health and relationship satisfaction does not mean that psychologically healthy men in midlife relinquish all aspects of the traditional male sex role. Studies of adult men consistently show that successful, healthy, happy middle-aged men possess many qualities of a traditional male gender role, such as being instrumentally competent, successful in their careers, and sexually active (Moreland, 1980).

Father-Adolescent Relationships

Erikson (1963, 1968) suggests that individuals during the middle years have the developmental task of resolving the conflict between generativity and stagnation. Generativity is primarily a concern for establishing and guiding the next generation. According to Erikson, generativity may be expressed in several ways: by nurturing and guiding one's own children, by mentoring and teaching others, or by deepening one's investment in work. In their study of adult men, Farrell and Rosenberg (1981) found that many men invest energy in fatherhood during middle age and increase their attempts to interact with their children. One interpretation of these findings is that this engagement is an attempt to resolve generativity issues during midlife.

According to both Erikson's ideas about the need to develop generativity and sex-role convergence theory, middle-aged men who develop intimate, expressive relations with their adolescent children should rate high on feelings of life satisfaction. The little research that exists on this issue supports the conclusion that fathers who are satisfied with their relations with their adolescents also report high feelings of well-being at midlife (Barnett, Marshall, and Pleck, 1992; McKenry, Arnold, Julian, and Kuo, 1987).

A renewed interest in relationships—or, for some fathers, a first-time interest—may not always lead to the development of a close and intimate father-adolescent relationship, however. Traditional fathers who emphasize achievement and suppression of affect may find it difficult to form close relations with adolescent children, which require a degree of cooperation and equality not found in earlier father-child relations. Furthermore, a desire to form a close relationship with the child in adolescence may occur for many middle-aged fathers at just the wrong time. Adolescents are also undergoing developmental changes, individuating from the family and investing more time and energy with friends. Thus fathers and adolescents may be on out-of-phase developmental trajectories leading to asynchronous relationships. Midlife may be an opportunity for fathers and adolescents to establish new or better relations, but it could also be a time of missed signals and differing interests, leading to a decrease in the quality of the father-adolescent relationship.

Little empirical research exists on factors related to variation in the quality of the father-adolescent relationship in nonclinic families. Based on evidence gathered from interview studies and anecdotal accounts, clinicians have identified and discussed several problems in the father-adolescent relationship. Given the nature of the evidence and the focus on problems, it is not surprising that the emphasis is on portraying father-adolescent relationship difficulties. It is not known how widespread these problems are, but, based on what is now a relatively large body of empirical research, serious father-adolescent relationship difficulties appear to be rare (Collins and Russell, 1991). By examining problems that some fathers have when their children reach adolescence, we highlight and bring to the fore issues that many fathers may experience, but to a lesser degree.

Some fathers report a sense of loss as their children enter early adolescence and begin spending less time at home and more time with friends, and they experience an even greater loss when their children move away from home (Lewis and Duncan, 1990). This feeling may be especially strong in middle-aged fathers who are highly invested in the father role (Martin, 1985). Gould (1972) reported that men in their early forties who indicated that their family, rather than work, had become the foundation of their identity reported frequent feelings of anxiety during their children's adolescence. The fathers in this group continued to be concerned about their adolescents while recognizing that there was little time or opportunity left to shape the behavior of their offspring.

Some middle-aged men experience difficulty with loss of control over their adolescent children. Lowenthal and Chiriboga (1972) suggest that some fathers feel abandoned and devalued by the growing independence of their adolescent children. Difficulty in relinquishing attachments may be especially strong among fathers who are highly invested in the father role (Lewis, Frenau, and Roberts, 1979). In particular, some fathers and daughters find it difficult to unravel the ties that bind a father to "daddy's little girl." In regard to sons, Farrell and Rosenberg (1981) argue that some men try to relive their own adolescence through the lives of their sons. Trying to compensate for earlier disappointments and failures, some of the fathers in their study pressured their adolescent sons to perform in areas that stressed the adolescent and led to father-adolescent conflict. Finally, Levinson (1978) contends that middle-aged men undergoing midlife stress become somewhat more introspective and self-focused. As a result, these men disengage from their children and become less responsive to their needs.

Little empirical research exists on the impact on fathers of children entering adolescence or of adolescents reaching young adulthood. We know little about how fathers in general experience these developmental transitions or about variation in this experience. Which fathers experience difficulty during this period and which fathers do not? What kind of father-child relationship is at risk for transitional stress? Although answers to these questions do not yet exist, the researchers and clinicians discussed earlier provide several hypotheses for investigation. Essentially, they argue that fathers experiencing midlife stress and fathers who are highly invested in their relationships with their children may be at risk for at least a temporary period of stress during the children's adolescence. Additionally, some authors point out that the period of adolescence, especially when it is a difficult period for the adolescent, may contribute to male midlife stress.

The Present Study

The purpose of the present study was to examine variation in the quality of father-adolescent communication. Communication was chosen for investigation because of its centrality in the parent-adolescent relationship. Our primary focus was on fathers, especially on midlife developmental changes that might alter a man's view of himself and influence the quality of communication with his adolescent. The main hypothesis in the study was that male midlife stress is negatively related to father-adolescent communication.

Three other factors thought to be related to the quality of father-adolescent communication and to the intensity of midlife stress also were examined in the present study. Of particular interest was the father's testosterone level. A large body of work has demonstrated positive correlations between testosterone levels and aggressive behavior in males in childhood and adolescence (Buchanan, Eccles, and Becker, 1992). Other research suggests that adult men with high levels of testosterone are more dominant and aggressive (Archer, 1991; Meyer-Bahlburg, 1981) and more likely to be arrested for spouse abuse (Lindman, von der Pahlen, Ost, and Eriksson, 1992). Together these findings suggest that testosterone is implicated in the expression of male dominance and aggression. Based on this idea, an exploratory hypothesis investigated in this study is that men high in testosterone have more traditional, more authoritarian, and thus less satisfying relations with their adolescents.

Two additional factors were expected to be related to the quality of communication with adolescents: fathers' marital satisfaction and their emotional expressiveness. Midlife is a time when many men are open and receptive to opportunities for greater involvement with their wives. We expect that a satisfying relationship with one's wife would attenuate midlife stress and lead to a deeper involvement with children, whereas an unsatisfying spousal relationship would exacerbate midlife stress and be associated with lower-quality father-adolescent relations. Finally, we expect that men who are emotionally expressive, who express their feelings rather than inhibit emotion, will have positive relations with their adolescent children.

Method

Subjects. Intra-office notices were sent to three large employment settings inviting men to participate in a study of men's job and family roles at midlife to increase knowledge about the ways men respond psychologically, socially, and physiologically to changes at midlife. To participate in the study each man had to be married, have a child between the ages of twelve and nineteen, not be taking any medication that might alter testosterone level, and not be obese. A $10 fee was offered for participation. A man who wanted to take part returned the contact letter with his signature, phone number, and address.

The sample in the present study consisted of thirty-seven middle-aged males between the ages of thirty-nine and fifty, with a mean age of 44.9 years. The majority of the men were white, Protestant, college graduates, and in good physical health. Data were collected on forty-one men. Three subjects were excluded from the analysis after it was discovered that they did not meet the criteria. Another subject was excluded from the analysis when it was discovered that he had the flu when his blood sample was obtained.

Testosterone level was assessed from a sample of blood drawn from each man between 9:00 A.M. and 10:00 A.M. The blood draw was performed at the same time for all men to control for circadian fluctuation on plasma testosterone levels. The men were instructed to refrain from exercising for twenty-four hours prior to the blood-sampling procedure. Following completion of the venipuncture, each man was given a questionnaire packet. Subjects had the option of completing the questionnaires immediately after the blood draw or completing them at their convenience.

Certain findings from these data are reported elsewhere (Julian and Mc-Kenry, 1989; Julian, McKenry, and Arnold, 1990; Julian, McKenry, and Mc-Kelvey, 1992).

Measures. The measurements derived from the study were based on subjects' responses according to a number of standard scales.

Mid-Life Crisis Scale. The Mid-Life Crisis Scale (Farrell and Rosenberg, 1981) was used to measure stress associated with midlife transition. The scale consists of twelve items designed to assess the degree to which a man is experiencing difficulty in coping with the stress of middle age. Questions are answered on a Likert scale. Questions include the following: "Marriage is as rewarding and enjoyable after 15 or 20 years as it is in the earlier years." "I find myself thinking about what kind of person I am and what I really want out of life."

Marital Comparison Level Index. The Marital Comparison Level Index (MCLI) (Sabatelli, 1984) was used to assess marital quality. The MCLI was designed to measure an individual's evaluation of the outcomes from his or her marital relationship in comparison with what was expected. The assumption behind the scale is that the less the outcomes from a relationship meet a person's expectations, the more complaints the person will have about the relationship. The scale consists of thirty-two items, derived from a review of past marital research, that reflect specific areas of concern in marital relationships.

Expression of Emotion Scale. The Expression of Emotion Scale (Balswick, 1979) was developed to measure the degree of emotion an individual expresses. According to Balswick the scale is useful in measuring "situational" emotionality and expressiveness. The scale consists of sixteen statements representing four subscales used to measure the expression of love, happiness, sadness, and hate. The scale consists of statement such as the following: "When I do feel love toward people I tell them." "When I do feel angry toward people I tell them."

Testosterone Level. In this study all of the serum testosterone samples were assayed together. The procedure used was a solid-phase radioimmunoassay. The amount of testosterone present in the study sample was determined from a standard curve. The 95 percent range of normal testosterone levels in this study of men at midlife was 3.6 to 9.9 nanograms per milliliter. The interassay variation was 7.9 percent for the test. The blood sample assay indicated that the men in this study were within the normal range of testosterone levels for adult males.

Parent-Adolescent Communication Scale. The Parent-Adolescent Communication Scale (Barnes and Olson, 1985) was used to measure the quality of the parent-adolescent relationship. This instrument was developed to assess a parent's perception and experience of communication with an adolescent. This self-report scale comprises twenty items in a Likert format. There are two subscales, each of which taps both content and process issues. The "open family communication" subscale is designed to assess positive aspects of parent-adolescent communication, and the "problems in family communication" subscale focuses on negative aspects of communication.

Results

The mean score on the Mid-Life Crisis Scale for this sample of men was $M = 3.74$, SD = 0.17. Based on normative data collected by Farrell and Rosenberg (1981), men within this range are satisfied with work and family roles and are generally optimistic about the future. Farrell and Rosenberg's "overt crisis" group had an average score of $M = 3.27$. Less than 5 percent of the men in the present study had scores equal to or below that mean.

Table 4.1 presents the correlation matrix for the variables included in the study. Quality of father-adolescent communication was significantly negatively correlated with fathers' midlife stress ($r = -.59$, $p < .01$) and testosterone level ($r = -.31$, $p < .05$) and positively correlated with emotional expressiveness ($r = .29$, $p < .05$).

The next step was to examine quality of father-adolescent communication as an outcome variable and use the other four variables as predictor variables (midlife stress, quality of marital relationship, emotional expressiveness, and testosterone level). A preliminary test indicated a lack of multicollinearity among the predictor variables. Stepwise multiple regression analysis revealed that all four predictor variables were significantly related to quality of father-adolescent communication ($F[5,37] = 7.86$, $R^2 = .51$, $p < .001$) and explained 51 percent of the variance. More specifically, less midlife stress, lower marital quality, greater emotional expressiveness, and lower testosterone level were significantly related to higher quality of father-adolescent communication. Midlife stress alone accounted for 37 percent of the variance in father-adolescent communication quality.

Discussion

Because data from the present study are correlational, it is not possible to make strong claims about causality. The purpose of this study was not to establish

Table 4.1. Correlation Matrix of Study Variables

Variable	2	3	4	5
(1) Midlife	−.24	−.15	−.06	−.59**
(2) Marital quality		.29*	−.24	−.17
(3) Emotional expressiveness			−.13	.29*
(4) Testosterone level				−.31
(5) Father-adolescent communication				

* $p < .05$
** $p < .01$

causality, however, but to account for variation in father-adolescent communication quality. It will take additional longitudinal research to identify the causal relations among the variables examined in this study. Such research is worthwhile, but contemporary conceptualizations of the parent-adolescent relationship focus less on unidirectional paths of causality from one individual to another and more on reciprocal influences within a relational context (see, for example, Collins and Repinski, in press). Future research needs to examine ways in which characteristics of fathers and characteristics of adolescents influence the development of the father-adolescent relationship, which in turn affects fathers and adolescents.

The magnitude of the correlations found in this investigation is noteworthy, given that this is a sample of reasonably homogeneous men who are well functioning. The range of scores for most of the variables was not wide. Few of the men were in a state of full-blown midlife crisis, virtually all were within the normal range of testosterone level, and communication between fathers and their adolescents generally was good. Yet despite this truncated range of scores, correlations of impressive magnitude were uncovered, indicating strong relations among the variables.

The strongest finding was the significant inverse correlation between male midlife stress and the quality of father-adolescent communication. There are at least two explanations for this association. A traditional explanation focuses on the impact of father midlife stress on father-adolescent relations. For example, according to Levinson (1978), a father experiencing midlife stress is preoccupied with personal identity issues and psychologically focused on his own interior life. As a result such a father has little interest in his adolescent, which leads to a decrease in time together and a decline in the quality of communication. An alternative interpretation views midlife stress as one outcome of father-adolescent relationship difficulties. A reasonable assumption about the middle-class professional men in this study is that they are psychologically invested in their children and incorporate fatherhood into their definition of themselves. For these fathers, communication difficulties with their adolescents may precipitate midlife stress. Whatever the direction of causality, data from this study and others (for example, Silverberg and Steinberg, 1990) suggest that adolescence may be an important context for the appearance of midlife concerns among fathers and mothers.

Fathers' emotional expressiveness was positively related to their assessment of the quality of father-adolescent communication. Emotional expressiveness is a measure of the degree to which fathers reveal their feelings, both positive and negative, to others. It is not surprising that fathers who report expressing positive emotions also report that they and their adolescents communicate well together. An impressive body of research demonstrates a positive relation between the expression of positive emotions and social functioning, including social and family relationships (Lazarus, 1991). In regard to the relation between positive affect and interpersonal communication, some have argued that these two processes are difficult to disentangle since what people in close relationships mean by good communication is the expression of positive affect (Blechman, 1990). It is harder to explain why the expression of negative emotions might also contribute to good communication. Some have argued that negative emotions, such as anger, do not necessarily interfere with communication, and sometimes they may even facilitate it and lead to relationship enhancement (Averill, 1982). Although not specifically focusing on negative emotions, Cooper (1988) has shown that disagreement and conflict can be part of effective parent-adolescent communication. Further research is needed on the relation between emotional expression and interpersonal communication.

Testosterone level was inversely related to the quality of father-adolescent communication. Serum testosterone has been shown to be associated with a low threshold for hostility and anger in adolescent boys (Olweus, 1980). A quick-to-anger style in a father would likely interfere with father-adolescent communication and the development of a close, intimate father-adolescent relationship. As compelling as this line of argument is, one should not assume the primacy of biological factors over social and psychological events. It is possible that even normal adolescent bickering and nattering in these basically well-functioning families is sufficient to elevate fathers' testosterone levels. In support of this hypothesis, research using male rhesus monkeys demonstrates that testosterone secretion can be influenced by social and environmental variables (Rose, Gordon, and Bernstein, 1972). An important implication from the data in the present study is that biological factors need to be examined not only for adolescents during puberty but also for parents.

The use of a small, nonrandom sample of professional men in this study means that considerable caution should be exercised in generalizing these findings to other men, especially to men who are not middle-class professionals. Some writers have suggested that male midlife stress is seen mainly in middle-class professionals and is the result of an overidentification with work and the establishment of an identity primarily based on one's career (Cytrynbaum and others, 1980). The inevitable vicissitudes of work and the cresting of a career put men who define themselves by their job, primarily the middle class, at risk for midlife stress. Men who view their work in more instrumental and external terms, an attitude more typical of blue-collar workers, may be less likely to experience midlife stress.

In spite of its limitations, this is one of the few studies to examine variation in father-adolescent communication. It is the first to focus on father midlife stress and to include physiological measures of father functioning. The important lesson to be drawn from this study is the necessity of including characteristics of fathers in our attempts to understand adolescent development and parent-adolescent relations.

References

Archer, J. "The Influence of Testosterone on Human Aggression." British Journal of Psychology, 1991, 82, 1–28.

Averill, J. R. Anger and Aggression. New York: Springer-Verlag, 1982.

Balswick, J. O. "The Inexpressive Male: Functional Conflict and Role Theory as Contrasting Explanation." Family Coordinator, 1979, 28, 331–336.

Barnes, H. L., and Olson, D. H. "Parent-Adolescent Communication and the Circumplex Model." Child Development, 1985, 56, 438–447.

Barnett, R. C., Marshall, N. L., and Pleck, J. H. "Men's Multiple Roles and Their Relationship to Men's Psychological Distress." Journal of Marriage and the Family, 1992, 54, 358–367.

Blechman, E. A. "A New Look at Emotions and the Family: A Model of Effective Family Communication." In E. A. Blechman (ed.), Emotions and the Family. Hillsdale, N.J.: Erlbaum, 1990.

Borland, D. C. "Research on Middle Age: An Assessment." Gerontologist, 1978, 18, 379–386.

Borland, D. C. "A Cohort Analysis Approach to the Empty-Nest Syndrome Among Three Ethnic Groups of Women: A Theoretical Position." Journal of Marriage and the Family, 1982, 44, 117–129.

Bowen, G. L., and Orthner, D. K. "Sex-Role Congruency and Marital Quality." Journal of Marriage and the Family, 1983, 45, 223–230.

Brim, O. G. "Theories of the Male Mid-Life Crisis." Counseling Psychologist, 1976, 6, 2–9.

Buchanan, C. M., Eccles, J. S., and Becker, J. B. "Are Adolescents the Victims of Raging Hormones: Evidence for Activational Effects of Hormones on Moods and Behavior at Adolescence." Psychological Bulletin, 1992, 111, 62–107.

Cohen, J. F. "Male Roles in Mid-Life." Family Coordinator, 1979, 28, 465–471.

Collins, W. A., and Repinski, D. J. "Relationships During Adolescence: Continuity and Change in Interpersonal Perspective." In R. Montemayor, G. R. Adams, and T. P. Gullotta (eds.), The Development of Personal Relationships During Adolescence. Newbury Park, Calif.: Sage, in press.

Collins, W. A., and Russell, G. "Mother-Child and Father-Child Relationships in Middle Childhood and Adolescence: A Developmental Analysis." Developmental Review, 1991, 11, 99–136.

Cooper, C. R. "Commentary: The Role of Conflict in Adolescent-Parent Relationships." In M. R. Gunnar and W. A. Collins (eds.), Development During the Transition to Adolescence. Hillsdale, N.J.: Erlbaum, 1988.

Cytrynbaum, S., Blum, L., Patrick, A., Stein, J., Wadner, D., and Wilk, C. "Midlife Development: A Personality and Social Systems Perspective." In L. W. Poon (ed.), Aging in the 1980's: Psychological Issues. Washington, D.C.: American Psychological Association, 1980.

Erikson, E. H. Childhood and Society. New York: Norton, 1963.

Erikson, E. H. Identity: Youth and Crisis. New York: Norton, 1968.

Farrell, M. P., and Rosenberg, S. D. Men at Midlife. Boston: Auburn House, 1981.

Gould, R. L. "The Phases of Adult Life: A Study in Developmental Psychology." American Journal of Psychiatry, 1972, 129, 521–531.

Gould, R. L. Transformations: Growth and Change in Adult Life. New York: Simon & Schuster, 1978.

Gutmann, D. L. The Country of Old Men: Cross-Cultural Studies in the Psychology of Later Life. Occasional Papers in Gerontology, no. 5. Ann Arbor: Institute of Gerontology, University of Michigan, 1969.

Gutmann, D. L. Reclaimed Powers: Toward a New Psychology of Men and Women in Later Years. New York: Basic Books, 1987.

Julian, T. W., and McKenry, P. C. "Relationship of Testosterone to Men's Family Functioning at Mid-Life." Aggressive Behavior, 1989, 15, 281–289.

Julian, T. W., McKenry, P. C., and Arnold, K. "Psychosocial Predictors of Stress Associated with Male Midlife Transition." Sex Roles, 1990, 22, 707–722.

Julian, T. W., McKenry, P. C., and McKelvey, M. W. "Mediators of Relationship Stress Between Middle-Aged Fathers and Their Adolescent Children." Journal of Genetic Psychology, 1992, 152, 381–386.

Jung, C. G. Modern Man in Search of a Soul. Orlando, Fla.: Harcourt Brace Jovanovich, 1933.

Keen, S. Fire in the Belly: On Being a Man. New York: Bantam, 1991.

Lazarus, R. S. Emotion and Adaptation. New York: Oxford, 1991.

Levinson, D. J. The Seasons of a Man's Life. New York: Knopf, 1978.

Lewis, R. A., and Duncan, S. F. "How Fathers Respond When Their Youth Leave Home." Prevention in Human Services, 1990, 9, 223–234.

Lewis, R. A., Frenau, P. J., and Roberts, C. L. "Fathers and the Post-Parental Transition." Family Coordinator, 1979, 27, 514–520.

Lindman, R., von der Pahlen, B., Ost, B., and Eriksson, C. P. "Serum Testosterone, Cortisol, Glucose, and Ethanol in Males Arrested in Spousal Abuse." Aggressive Behavior, 1992, 18, 393–400.

Livson, F. B. "Paths to Psychological Health in the Middle Years: Sex Differences." In D. H. Eichorn, N. Haan, J. A. Clausen, M. P. Honzik, and P. H. Mussen (eds.), Present and Past in Middle Life. New York: Academic Press, 1981.

Lowenthal, M. F., and Chiriboga, D. "Transition to the Empty Nest: Crisis, Challenge, or Relief?" Archives of General Psychiatry, 1972, 26, 8–14.

Lowenthal, M. F., Thurnher, M., and Chiriboga, D. Four Stages of Life. San Francisco: Jossey-Bass, 1975.

McKenry, P. C., Arnold, K. D., Julian, T. W., and Kuo, J. "Interpersonal Influences on the Well-being of Men at Mid-Life." Family Perspective, 1987, 21, 225–233.

Martin, D. H. "Fathers and Adolescents." In S. M. Hanson and F. W. Boset (eds.), Dimensions of Fatherhood. Newbury Park, Calif.: Sage, 1985.

Meyer-Bahlburg, H. F. "Androgens and Human Aggression." In B. F. Brain and D. Benton (eds.), The Biology of Aggression. Rockville, Md.: Sijthoff & Noordhoff, 1981.

Moreland, J. "Age and Change in the Adult Male Sex Role." Sex Roles, 1980, 6, 807–818.

Neugarten, B. L. Middle Age and Aging. Chicago: University of Chicago Press, 1968.

Neugarten, B. L., and Gutmann, D. L. "Age-Sex Roles and Personality in Middle Age: A Thematic Apperception Study." Psychology Monographs, 1958, 72, 1–33.

Olweus, D. "Familial and Temperamental Determinants of Aggressive Behavior in Adolescent Boys: A Causal Analysis." Developmental Psychology, 1980, 16, 644–660.

Pleck, J. H. The Myth of Masculinity. Cambridge, Mass.: MIT Press, 1981.

Rose, R. M., Gordon, T. P., and Bernstein, I. S. "Plasma Testosterone Levels in Male Rhesus Monkeys: Influence of Sexual and Social Stimuli." Science, 1972, 178, 643–645.

Sabatelli, R. M. "The Marital Comparison Level Index: A Measure for Assessing Outcomes Relative to Expectations." Journal of Marriage and the Family, 1984, 46, 651–662.

Sheehy, G. Passages: Predictable Crises of Adult Life. New York: Bantam, 1976.

Silverberg, S. B., and Steinberg, L. "Psychological Well-being with Early Adolescent Children." Developmental Psychology, 1990, 26, 658–666.

Tamir, L. M. Men in Their Forties: The Transition to Middle Age. New York: Springer, 1982.

Vaillant, G. E. Adaptation to Life. Boston: Little, Brown, 1977.

RAYMOND MONTEMAYOR is associate professor of psychology at The Ohio State University.

PATRICK C. MCKENRY is professor of family relations and human development and adjunct professor of Black studies at The Ohio State University.

TERESA JULIAN is assistant professor in the College of Nursing at The Ohio State University.

Familistic values in recent immigrant families are linked to distinctive patterns of communication between adolescents and their fathers, mothers, and peers.

Values and Communication of Chinese, Filipino, European, Mexican, and Vietnamese American Adolescents with Their Families and Friends

*Catherine R. Cooper, Harley Baker,
Dina Polichar, Mara Welsh*

American psychologists have often defined maturity in terms of individualistic qualities such as autonomy, independence, and initiative, and consequently they have defined well-functioning families as preparing children for these ideals. Yet anthropological and sociological writings emphasize that many cultural traditions, including Asian, Latino, African, and Eastern and Southern European, accord a central role to familism—norms of collective support, allegiance, and obligation. In such traditions, good children show support, respect, and reticence in the family, especially toward their fathers. Achievement or failure brings pride or shame to the family as a whole rather than signifying autonomy or independence of an individual family member. This paper addresses familistic values among adolescents from a range of cultural

The work reported here was made possible by grants from the Faculty Senate of the University of California at Santa Cruz. The support of the National Center for Research in Cultural Diversity and Second Language Learning and the Bilingual Research Group at the University of California at Santa Cruz is gratefully acknowledged. We appreciate the contributions of Carolyn Cherry, Jill Denner, Shantel Forstall, Nancy Fu, Yasmeen Husain, Cynthia Miranda, Michael Moon, Christina Poulo, Jose Vergara, and Emily Wu to the research design and data collection; of Tom Tutco, Randy Craig, and Edward Lopez to data collection; of David Cooper and Xavier Tapias to data analysis; and of Margarita Azmitia, Robert Cooper, Per Gjerde, and Cam Leaper to conceptual development. Finally, we thank the research participants for their reflections and help throughout this work.

traditions and describes how individuality and connectedness are expressed within adolescents' family and peer relationships when cultural values emphasize the familistic qualities of respect and cohesion.

The theoretical perspective of this work focuses on the interplay between individuality and connectedness in the ongoing mutual regulation involved in relationships. Rather than framing individualism and collectivism as mutually exclusive cultural characteristics, the core of our model is the proposition that central to all relationships is the transactive interplay of individuality and connectedness, which functions as an important mechanism for both individual and relational development (Cooper, Grotevant, and Condon, 1983; Grotevant and Cooper, 1986). Individuality refers to processes that reflect the distinctiveness of the self. In language it is seen in assertions, disclosures, and disagreements with others. Connectedness involves processes that link the self to others, seen in acknowledgment of, respect for, and responsiveness to others. Our analyses of the conversations of families of European American adolescents revealed that family communication reflecting the interplay of both individuality and connectedness was associated with adolescents' identity development and role-taking skill (Cooper, Grotevant, and Condon, 1983; Grotevant and Cooper, 1986). A second proposition of the model, which has come to be known as the continuity hypothesis, is that children's and adolescents' experiences in family relationships regarding the interplay of individuality and connectedness carry over to attitudes, expectations, and skills beyond the family to relationships with peers. Among European American adolescents we observed different styles of communication with parents and peers, yet individual differences among adolescents in the interplay of individuality and connectedness with parents were related to such individual differences with peers (Cooper and Cooper, 1992).

Our more recent work with the individuality and connectedness model is consistent with the increasing interest in developmental theory in grounding the frame of reference in cultural terms, by moving away from considering children and adolescents in terms of static demographic categories and global ethnic group "characteristics" toward viewing individuals, families, and cultures as developing through time (Skolnick, Baumrind, and Bronson, 1990). We have been especially interested in the transaction of individuality and connectedness within family relationships when cultural traditions emphasize norms of respect and cohesion, and in how these traditions are powerful yet dynamic, changing in the process of immigration, acculturation, and economic mobility. Our approach has been extensively informed by current ecocultural theories (Weisner, Gallimore, and Jordan, 1988), which propose multidimensional models of the ecocultural niches of children and their relationships. Such models specify the goals and values of socialization; key personnel involved in socialization; the scripts or patterns of communication, both verbal and nonverbal; and features of activity settings in which important cultural information is transmitted. We have found the analysis of these features helpful in "unpackaging" accounts of the role of culture in development. This paper focuses particularly on the first three of these dimensions; other reports focus on the activity settings of school and household work (for example, Azmitia, Cooper, and Garcia, 1992; Cooper and others, in press; Cooper, Jackson, and Azmitia, in press).

Familistic Values

Because familistic values have been defined in many ways, they have been measured by questions tapping various features, including shared family goals, common property, mutual support, and the desire to perpetuate the family (Bardis, 1959). Familistic values have also been considered adaptive resources for ethnic families of color, especially under conditions of racism, immigration, or poverty (Harrison and others, 1990). Comparative studies have reported that Mexican Americans, Central Americans, and Cuban Americans have endorsed norms of familial obligation, family support, and use of the family as reference group, with family support showing the greatest stability across generations after immigration to the United States (Sabogal and others, 1987). Similar cultural values are evident in reports of traditional Chinese culture and Confucian values, which emphasize both family harmony, including social etiquette and face-saving communication among family members, and respect for family hierarchy, marked by conformity and obedience to those in authority (Hong, 1989; White and Chan, 1983). These values have been found to persist even as Chinese immigrants have experienced declining patrilineal kinship, scattering of extended families, and increased reliance on fictive kinship (Wong, 1985). Vietnamese ancestral worship and patrilineal traditions have been described in similar terms. Although disproportionately fewer elderly Vietnamese are with their families in the United States, kinship patterns appear stable among recent immigrants, and those who have been able to retain kinship are considered to be making better adjustments than those without such ties (Dunning, 1986; Haines, 1988; Masuda, Lin, and Tazuma, 1980). As with other cultural groups, Filipino traditions of familistic values, including norms of mutual support and hierarchical patterns of authority, have been described as pervasive yet undergoing changes among recent immigrants to the United States (Santos, 1983).

Adolescents' Communication with Families and Peers

Familistic values emphasizing mutual support and the authority of parents—especially fathers—are reflected in distinctive patterns of communicating individuality and connectedness. For example, decisions that are considered to lie within adolescents' personal jurisdiction of "identity" in European American middle-class families, such as those regarding educational, career, dating, and marital choices, may be made by the head of the household in recently immigrated families (Santos, 1983). Fathers' relationships with their adolescents may thus be more hierarchical, resulting in low levels of consultation and negotiation with other family members. Accounts of Chinese and Anglo-Chinese parents valuing both conformity and self-direction in their children (Lin and Fu, 1990) are consistent with cultural traditions emphasizing harmony and tact, in which people are expected to sense one another's needs without explicit communication and to convey their own feelings with indirectness and subtlety.

Like familistic values, however, traditional communication patterns show signs of change. Economic necessity may effect a reorganization of family living patterns to accommodate shifting patterns of parental employment. For example, Davis and Chavez (1985) have described role reversals within Hispanic families in which unemployed men assume greater responsibility for household maintenance while their wives work outside the home. In other cases, changing marital roles may reflect adoption of middle-class democratic and egalitarian values (Gibbs, 1989).

The present study was designed to assess the role of ecocultural dimensions in adolescents' relationships with families—including fathers, mothers, and siblings—as well as with peers, by investigating three questions. First, what distinctive cultural patterns occur in familistic values among adolescents and their fathers and mothers, including patterns of intergenerational continuity and change? We investigated whether adolescents from cultural groups with more recent immigration experiences might be more likely to endorse familistic values than would European American adolescents, and also whether adolescents would be more likely to attribute familistic values to their parents than to themselves.

Second, we investigated what distinctive cultural patterns might occur in scripts or patterns of communication reflecting individuality and connectedness between adolescents and their families and peers. On the basis of earlier research, we predicted higher levels of expressions of individuality with parents among European descent adolescents than among those for whom cultural norms of respect might make the expression of assertions, disagreements, and disclosures less common. We also investigated the degree to which hierarchical patterns of decision making are evident in parent-adolescent communication.

Third, within each cultural group, we investigated whether adolescents' expressions of individuality and connectedness with their fathers, mothers, and siblings may be differentially related to communication with their friends on a range of practical and personal topics typical of adolescents' activities and interests. On the basis of the continuity model, we predicted that when norms of respect render adolescents' relations with parents more formal, siblings may become more important links to adolescents' peer relationships across activity settings. We also predicted that continuity rather than compensation would be reflected in the associations between family and peer communication patterns (Cooper and Cooper, 1992).

In this study we made three important methodological changes from our earlier observational work on adolescents' family and peer discourse (Cooper and Cooper, 1992; Cooper, Grotevant, and Condon, 1983; Grotevant and Cooper, 1986). First, since we wanted to consider variability within each group, we used methods that would allow a larger sample than those typical of labor-intensive discourse studies. Second, because we sought to understand the expression of individuality and connectedness in families where norms of respect, particularly toward fathers, might make overt expressions of individuality rare, we chose self-report rather than observational methods to explore what does not happen as well as what does. Finally, throughout our work, we consulted focus groups composed of adolescents from each cultural group studied to make our instrument development, data analysis, and interpretations consistent with their experiences in family and peer relationships.

Method

Research Participants. The college students in our northern California sample identified themselves in terms of over thirty ethnic categories. This paper concerns the 393 adolescents who described themselves as of Mexican ($N = 96$), Vietnamese ($N = 38$), Filipino ($N = 56$), Chinese ($N = 58$), and European descent ($N = 145$) in response to questions about the ethnicity and country of origin for themselves and each family member. Adolescents in each group were of comparable ages ($M = 19.9$ years). The remaining adolescents in the sample included approximately 10 percent multiple-heritage youth as well as others in numbers too small for the analyses conducted for this paper. A high percentage of the adolescents in the sample were themselves immigrants, with 27 percent of Mexican, 52 percent of Chinese, 50 percent of Filipino, 84 percent of Vietnamese, and 5 percent of European descent adolescents being first-generation immigrants. Large proportions of the remaining students in the first four groups were children of immigrants. According to adolescents' reports, parents of Mexican descent adolescents had lower levels of formal education than parents in other groups, although unemployment appeared to be highest among parents of Vietnamese adolescents.

Measures. Adolescents rated the degree to which they perceived a set of familistic values to be held by themselves, their mothers, their fathers, and their maternal and paternal grandparents. This list, adapted from those used in studies of Hispanic and Asian acculturation, assesses the extent to which the family is seen as a source of support and obligation and as a reference group for decision making. Sample items include the following (Sabogal and others, 1987): "Family members should make sacrifices to guarantee a good education for their children." "Older siblings should help directly support other family members economically." "Much of what a son or daughter does in life should be done to please parents." "Families should consult close relatives, such as uncles and aunts, concerning what they see as important decisions."

Adolescents also characterized their expressions of individuality and connectedness with their mothers, fathers, siblings, same-gender friends, and opposite-gender friends by rating descriptive statements such as: "When I disagree with this person I try to negotiate." "This person communicates openly with me about his/her feelings." "I discuss my problems with this person." Finally, they rated how comfortable they felt discussing a number of topics, including how well they were doing in school; career goals; sexuality, dating, and marriage; ethnicity and culture; moral values; and alcohol and drugs. For the purposes of this paper, only illustrative patterns are presented; a more extensive presentation of findings will appear in a forthcoming volume (Cooper, in press).

Results and Discussion

Familistic Values. Adolescents' responses to questions about familistic values demonstrate the multidimensional nature of this construct. For example, on the average, adolescents from all five cultural groups strongly endorsed the statement "Family members should make sacrifices to guarantee a good education for their children," with no mean differences among groups (M = 3.60 [on 4-point scale, with 1 = disagree, 2 = somewhat disagree, 3 = somewhat agree, and 4 = agree], SD = 0.64, $F[4,322] = 1.86$, n.s.). Thus at one level of analysis, adolescents from all five groups could be considered to hold familistic values. However, adolescents from these groups differed in their endorsement of a statement expressing norms of mutual support among siblings: "Older siblings should help directly support other family members economically." Chinese, Filipino, Mexican, and Vietnamese American adolescents endorsed this statement more strongly than did European American adolescents ($F[4,313] = 17.95$, $p < .001$). Adolescents of Filipino and Mexican descent reported endorsing this value less than their parents, whereas adolescents of Vietnamese and Chinese descent reported sharing parents' strong endorsement and European Americans reported sharing parents' weak endorsement of this value.

The use of the family as a reference group in decision making was tapped by statements such as "Much of what a son or daughter does in life should be done to please the parents." Chinese, Filipino, Mexican, and Vietnamese descent adolescents reported that they and their parents endorsed this value more than did European descent adolescents ($F[4,307] = 11.35$, $p < .001$) but across the five cultural groups significant main effects for generation were also found, with adolescents reporting their parents endorsing this more strongly than they did ($F[2,584] = 79.50$, $p \leq .001$).

A similar pattern of differences among cultural groups as well as between generations was found for a related item: "The family should consult close relatives such as uncles and aunts concerning what they see as important decisions." Chinese, Filipino, and Vietnamese descent students endorsed this value significantly more than both Mexican and European descent students (F[4,304]= 4.68, p < .001, but adolescents in all groups viewed their parents as holding this value significantly more strongly than they did. No significant differences were found in adolescents' views of their fathers' versus mothers' expectations or between male and female adolescents.

Thus Mexican, Chinese, Vietnamese, and Filipino descent adolescents in our sample tended to endorse familistic values regarding mutual support among siblings as well as turning to parents and other close relatives in making important decisions. These findings document the strength of these values among adolescents in our sample, many of whom represented either the first or the second generation in the United States, yet we also found significant intergenerational differences. These findings suggest both continuity and change in familistic values in the groups sampled.

Communication with Families and Peers. A key finding regarding adolescents' descriptions of their communication was that within each cultural group, adolescents reported more formal communication with their fathers and more open communication of individuality and more negotiation with their mothers, siblings, and friends. For example, in response to the statements "This person communicates openly with me about his/her feelings" and "I discuss my problems with this person," adolescents in each of the five cultural groups reported lower agreement with respect to their fathers than to their mothers, siblings, or friends (F[4,280] = 38.42, p < .0001, and F[4,274] = 33.23, p < .001, respectively) (see Figures 5.1 and 5.2). With regard to hierarchical patterns of communication, adolescents were most likely to agree that their fathers, compared with other family members or friends, "make most of the decisions in our relationship" (F[4,289] = 54.252, p < .0001) (see Figure 5.3). Chinese, Filipino, and Vietnamese descent adolescents endorsed this description of their relationships with their fathers significantly more than did adolescents of Mexican and European descent.

The importance of context in understanding adolescents' communication with family and peers can be seen in their rating of how comfortable they felt talking with their fathers, mothers, siblings, and same- and opposite-gender friends on two contrasting topics: sexuality, dating, and marriage; and how well they were doing in school. For these topics, they rated statements of the form "I feel comfortable talking about X with this person," with 1 = disagree, 2 = somewhat disagree, 3 = somewhat agree, and 4 = agree. As shown in Table 5.1, effects of relationship, cultural group, and interactions were found for both topics.

On the topic of sexuality, dating, and marriage, adolescents in all five cultural groups reported what we will term a "gradient of comfort," feeling the least comfort with fathers and progressively more with mothers, siblings, and friends. Chinese and Vietnamese American students reported feeling less comfort than Filipino and Mexican American students, who in turn felt less comfort than European American students. In absolute terms, Filipino, Mexican,

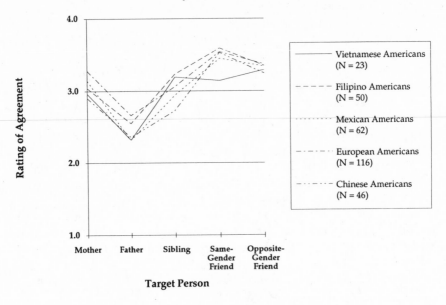

Figure 5.1. Mean Ratings by Adolescents of the Statement
"This Person Communicates Openly with Me About His/Her Feelings"
for Family Members and Friends

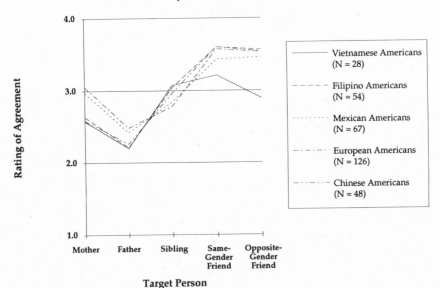

Figure 5.2. Mean Ratings by Adolescents of the Statement
"I Discuss My Problems with This Person"
for Family Members and Friends

**Figure 5.3. Mean Ratings by Adolescents of the Statement
"This Person Makes Most of the Decisions in Our Relationship"
for Family Members and Friends**

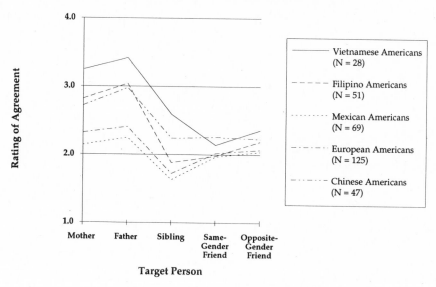

and European American students, on the average, reported feeling comfortable discussing sexuality, dating, and marriage with their mothers, whereas Chinese and Vietnamese American students reported feeling somewhat uncomfortable.

On the topic of how well they were doing in school, adolescents in all groups reported a similar comfort gradient, with progressively greater levels of comfort from fathers to mothers and siblings to friends. On the average, adolescents in all groups reported feeling comfortable talking with their fathers.

It is striking that adolescents in some cultural groups expressed high levels of familistic values concerning support and reliance on the advice of family members, but felt some discomfort in actually discussing some topics. In follow-up focus groups held separately with adolescents from each cultural group, students confirmed their experience of holding familistic values and turning to their families for advice, together with holding formal relationships with fathers. They elaborated that they might discuss school with their fathers, but that the salience of their fathers' authority might lead them not to disclose sensitive facts such as having changed their undergraduate major from premed to humanities or social science. These remarks suggest that issues of reasoning, judgment, and negotiation of personal and parental jurisdiction continue to be salient in late adolescence (Yau and Smetana, in press). Some students remarked that they felt they might convey such information to their fathers through their mothers, siblings, or cousins (see Youniss and Smollar, 1985).

Table 5.1. Adolescents' Comfort Levels When Talking with Family Members and Friends

"I feel comfortable talking about sexuality, dating, and marriage with this person."

Target Person	Vietnamese Americans (N = 24)	Filipino Americans (N = 42)	Mexican Americans (N = 63)	Eropean Americans (N = 116)	Chinese Americans (N = 47)	Overall Mean (N = 292)
Father	1.58	1.93	1.86	2.26	1.70	1.97 (a)
Mother	1.88	2.12	2.52	2.71	1.98	2.44 (b)
Sibling	2.92	2.74	2.76	2.99	2.51	2.82 (c)
Same-gender friend	3.29	3.62	3.43	3.67	3.38	3.53 (d)
Opposite-gender friend	2.96	3.64	3.44	3.57	3.36	3.47 (d)
Overall means	2.53 (e)	2.79 (e,f)	2.80 (e,f)	3.06 (f)	2.59 (e)	

"I feel comfortable talking about how well I'm doing in school with this person."

Target Person	Vietnamese Americans (N = 24)	Filipino Americans (N = 42)	Mexican Americans (N = 63)	Eropean Americans (N = 116)	Chinese Americans (N = 47)	Overall Mean (N = 292)
Father	2.54	2.67	3.00	3.26	2.70	2.97 (a)
Mother	2.79	3.02	3.22	3.41	2.85	3.17 (b)
Sibling	3.08	3.12	3.18	3.30	3.30	3.23 (b)
Same-gender friend	3.13	3.17	3.40	3.55	3.38	3.40 (c)
Opposite-gender friend	3.13	3.31	3.41	3.56	3.49	3.44 (c)
Overall means	2.93 (e)	3.06 (e,f)	3.24 (e,f)	3.41 (f)	3.14 (e,f)	

Note: Rows and columns labeled with different letters differ at the .05 level based on Newman-Keuls post-hoc tests.

This view appeared more common among immigrant youth, several of whom described their own roles as that of "the third parent."

Links Between Adolescents' Communication with Family and Peers. Our findings provide some support for the continuity model and for the hypothesis that when norms of respect render adolescents' relationships with parents more formal, siblings may function as important links to adolescents' peer relationships. As shown in Figure 5.4, on the topic of sexuality, dating, and marriage—for which adolescents' communication with parents, especially fathers, was less open—significant correlations were found between adolescents' comfort in communicating with their siblings and friends among Filipino, Mexican, and European descent adolescents. In contrast, as shown in Figure 5.5, on the topic of how well they were doing in school, adolescents' ratings of comfort in talking with friends were associated with ratings of siblings and mothers for Filipino, Mexican, European, and Vietnamese descent adolescents and with ratings of fathers for Filipino, Mexican, and European descent adolescents.

These findings suggest that linkages between family and peer relationships may differ across cultural groups as well as across topics or activity settings. For example, in talking about school, Mexican American adolescents' views of their fathers, mothers, and siblings were all associated with their views of

**Figure 5.4. Correlations Between Adolescents' Comfort
in Talking About Sexuality, Dating, and Marriage
with Family Members and with Friends**

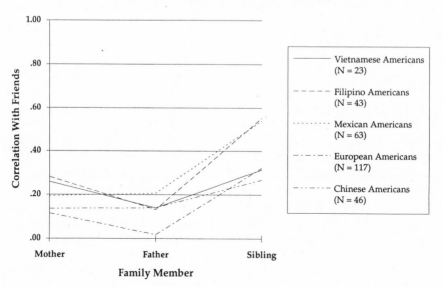

Figure 5.5. Correlations Between Adolescents' Comfort in Talking About How Well They Are Doing in School with Family Members and with Friends

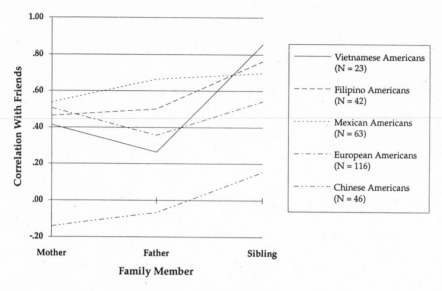

friends, whereas Chinese American adolescents' ratings reflected no significant associations between adolescents' views of family and peers.

Conclusions and Next Steps

These findings regarding values and communication in adolescents' relationships with family and peers appear to challenge definitions of adolescent maturity solely in terms of autonomy. They also enrich the model of individuality and connectedness by clarifying the significance of distinctive personnel in adolescents' lives, including fathers, mothers, and siblings; values regarding mutual family support and guidance; and patterns of communication in the context of discussing particular topics. In the present study, adolescents from Chinese, Filipino, Mexican, and Vietnamese families saw themselves and their parents as holding norms of reliance on family members for both support and guidance in decision making. Patterns of communication generally appeared more formal with fathers than with mothers in all cultural groups, with hierarchical patterns especially evident within Asian American families. Our analyses of the association between family and peer communication patterns provide some support for the continuity model and the hypothesis that when norms of respect render adolescents' relations with parents more formal, siblings may become more important in contributing to adolescents' peer relational skills. However, they also indicate that linkages between families and peers may vary in different cultural groups as well as domains.

In our focus group discussions, adolescents from several cultural groups described how their fathers' expectations and opinions were often conveyed to them by their mothers, and how their mothers' expectations were often conveyed to them by siblings or cousins. Hence in our current work we are investigating the contributions of fathers and other family members to adolescent maturity in ways that go beyond dyadic relationships and direct talk. In a study of Mexican American and European American children and adolescents, interviews of fathers and mothers in their homes in their native languages have revealed the indirect ways in which both parents convey their values and contribute to the guidance of their children, especially when domains of expertise differ between generations (Azmitia, Cooper, and Garcia, 1992). In a study of Japanese, Japanese American, and European American adolescents, conducted in collaboration with our Japanese colleagues Hiroshi Azuma, Keiko Kashiwagi, Hiroshi Shimizu, and Otoshi Suzuki, we are investigating how values and expectations are conveyed and we are probing the indirect pathways of guidance and negotiation of both fathers and mothers (Gjerde and Cooper, 1992). We are also investigating "bridges and buffers" in the patterns of linkages among families, peers, school, and work that reflect a range of continuities and discontinuities, rather than assuming that continuities or "matches" between developmental contexts are necessarily positive (Azmitia, Cooper, and Garcia, 1991; Cooper, Jackson, and Azmitia, in press).

Useful Strategies for Studying Culture and Development

We conclude by noting four ways in which conceptions of culture and relationships have enriched our research strategies. First, we wish to underscore the importance of collaboration among colleagues, students, and research participants with a range of cultural experiences. This is especially important given the danger of using middle-class European American experiences as models of universal patterns of development, proceeding to use research constructs and instruments derived from one culture with members of another culture, and interpreting between-culture differences as deficits compared with middle-class European American experience. A useful framework for this progressive collaboration is the "parallel research" design described by Sue and Sue (1987). In this approach, investigators first identify potentially universal processes, such as those involved in family guidance, negotiation, and conflict resolution as adolescents come to maturity (Cooper, in press). Investigators then develop ways to measure those processes that are appropriate for each culture studied and then identify both similarities and differences across cultural groups in terms of how these processes contribute to adolescent development.

Second, taking a developmental view of individuals, relationships, and cultures as dynamic rather than static and monolithic is reflected in the method of assessing adolescents' cultural or ethnic identity with open-ended questions rather than requiring them to check one of a set of predetermined self-descriptions. When Stephan (1992) used such open-ended questions, she found multiple-heritage identities among adolescents within many ethnic "groups," and she also found situational variation in the self-descriptions they used when completing official forms; describing how they saw themselves with their families, classmates, and friends; and naming the group with whom they identified most closely. In the present study, open-ended response formats also revealed evidence of these multiple-heritage and situational patterns of ethnic identity. We found that our sample included about 10 percent multiple-heritage youth, and that a number of adolescents described both their parents as Chinese and reported speaking Mandarin with them yet listed their own ethnicity as Vietnamese, apparently reflecting their experiences as refugees. Similar issues emerge with regard to describing family composition. Students asked us: "What do I put under mother and father if I was raised by my grandmother and never knew my mother or father?" "My aunt is like a sister to me—are you going to ask about her?" "What if I'm like the third parent in my family?" These examples illustrate how ethnicity and family are culturally and socially constructed meanings, and how we might adapt our research methods to enrich our understanding of them (see Cooper, Jackson, and Azmitia, in press, for further discussion of these issues).

Third, rather than pursuing idealized representative samples, it may be more useful to provide "ballpark" descriptions of parameters of samples linked to key ecocultural dimensions, such as communities of origin, generation and goals of immigration, family structure and membership, and languages spoken (Schofield and Anderson, 1989). Finally, self-report and observational methodologies have each made important contributions to cultural research on development. Open-ended interviews with individuals and with focus groups are critical for overcoming ethnocentrism and the inevitable limitations of any one investigator's cultural experiences; survey methods are critical for assessing generalizability across diverse populations; and observational work, including discourse analyses, provides insight about transactive relational patterns that individuals may be unaware of and hence unable to report.

In closing, we note that our findings have stimulated us to reconsider views of parents and adolescents as progressively renegotiating asymmetrical patterns of parent-child regulation toward peerlike mutuality. Such accounts may be better descriptions of European American families than of recent immigrants whose traditions sustain more hierarchical patterns, but we may benefit from examining more closely how individuality and connectedness are negotiated across generations in any cultural group. Even accounts of European American fathers suggest challenges in this process. For example, the "bridge hypothesis" of Mannle and Tomasello is based on Gleason's (1975, p. 293) proposal that, during language acquisition, "fathers are not as well tuned in to their children as mothers are in the traditional family situation. . . . There are probably serious and far-reaching good effects that result. . . . Children have to learn to talk to their fathers and other strangers. . . . (They) try harder to make themselves both heard and understood. In this way, fathers can be seen as a bridge to the outside world, leading the child to change her or his language in order to be understood" (cited in Mannle and Tomasello, 1987, p. 24).

A different sort of fathers' bridging was described in a focus group held recently in Japan, when a college student told our colleagues how their father wanted her to work at his company so he could see her more often. Hence we extend the remarks of Collins and Russell (1991) by observing that communicative challenges may exist between adolescents and their families and friends from a range of cultural groups, but understanding variability within and between groups in how such challenges are met will help us map key resources for adolescents' coming to maturity.

References

Azmitia, M., Cooper, C. R., and Garcia, E. E. "Bridging Home, School and Community: Implications for the Educational Achievement of Low-Income Mexican American and European American Children." Paper presented at the meetings of the American Educational Research Association, San Francisco, 1992.

Bardis, P. D. "A Familism Scale." Marriage and Family Living, 1959, 13, 340–341.

Collins, W. A., and Russell, G. "Mother-Child and Father-Child Relationships in Middle Childhood and Adolescence: A Developmental Analysis." Developmental Review, 1991, 11, 99–136.

Cooper, C. R. The Weaving of Maturity: Cultural Perspectives on Adolescent Development. New York: Oxford University Press, in press.

Cooper, C. R., Azmitia, M., Garcia, E. E., Ittel, A., Lopez, E., Rivera, L., and Martinez-Chavez, R. "I Would Like Her to Get to College, but the Way Things Are Now, Who Knows?": Aspirations of Low-Income Mexican American and European American Parents for Their Children. In F. A. Villarruel and R. M. Lerner (eds.), Environments for Socialization and Learning. New Directions in Child Development, no. 63. San Francisco: Jossey-Bass, in press.

Cooper, C. R., and Cooper, R. G. "Links Between Adolescents' Relationships with Their Parents and Peers: Models, Evidence, and Mechanisms." In R. D. Parke and G. W. Ladd (eds.), Family-Peer Relationships: Modes of Linkages. Hillsdale, N.J.: Erlbaum, 1992.

Cooper, C. R., Grotevant, H. D., and Condon, S. M. "Individuality and Connectedness in the Family as a Context for Adolescent Identity Formation and Role Taking Skill." In H. D. Grotevant and C. R. Cooper (eds.), Adolescent Development in the Family. New Directions in Child Development, no. 22. San Francisco: Jossey-Bass, 1983.

Cooper, C. R., Jackson, J. F., and Azmitia, M. "Bridging Multiple Worlds: African American and Latino Youth in Academic Outreach Programs." In V. McLoyd and L. Steinberg (eds.), Conceptual and Methodological Issues in the Study of Minority Adolescents and Their Families. In press.

Davis, S. K., and Chavez, V. "Hispanic Househusbands." Hispanic Journal of Behavioral Sciences, 1985, 7, 317–332.

Dunning, B. B. "Vietnamese in America: Domain and Scope of Adjustment Among 1975–1979 Arrivals." Paper presented at the meetings of the American Association for the Advancement of Science, Philadelphia, 1986.

Gibbs, J. T. "Black American Adolescents." In J. T. Gibbs, L. N. Huang, and Associates, Children of Color: Psychological Interventions with Minority Youth. San Francisco: Jossey-Bass, 1989.

Gjerde, P. F., and Cooper, C. R. Family Influences in Japan and the U.S.: Between and Within-Cultural Analyses of Ecocultural Niches. Santa Cruz: University of California Pacific Rim Foundation, 1992.

Gleason, J. B. "Fathers and Other Strangers: Men's Speech to Young Children." In Georgetown University Roundtable on Language and Linguistics. Washington, D.C.: Georgetown University Press, 1975.

Grotevant, H. D., and Cooper, C. R. "Individuation in Family Relationship: A Perspective on Individual Differences in the Development of Identity and Role Taking in Adolescence." Human Development, 1986, 29, 82–100.

Haines, D. W. "Kinship in Vietnamese Refugee Resettlement: A Review of the U.S. Experience." Journal of Comparative Family Studies, 1988, 19, 1–16.

Harrison, A. O., Wilson, M. N., Pine, C. J., Chan, S. Q., and Buriel, R. "Family Ecologies of Ethnic Minority Children." Child Development, 1990, 61, 347–362.

Hong, G. K. "Application of Cultural and Environmental Issues in Family Therapy with Immigrant Chinese Americans." Journal of Strategic and Systematic Therapies, 1989, 8, 14–21.

Lin, C.Y.C., and Fu, V. R. "A Comparison of Child-Rearing Practices Among Chinese, Immigrant Chinese, and Caucasian-American Parents." Child Development, 1990, 61, 429–433.

Mannle, S., and Tomasello, M. "Fathers, Siblings, and the Bridge Hypothesis." In K. E. Nelson and A. Van Kleeck (eds.), Children's Language. Vol. 6. Hillsdale, N.J.: Erlbaum, 1987.

Masuda, M., Lin, K.-M., and Tazuma, L. "Adaptation Problems of Vietnamese Refugees: Life Changes and Perception of Life Events." Archives of General Psychiatry, 1980, 37, 447–450.

Sabogal, F., Marin, G., Otero-Sabogal, R., Marin, B. V., and Perez-Stable, E. J. "Hispanic Familism and Acculturation: What Changes and What Doesn't?" Hispanic Journal of Behavioral Sciences, 1987, 9, 397–412.

Santos, R. A. "The Social and Emotional Development of Filipino-American Children." In G. J. Powell, J. Yamamoto, A. Romero, and A. Morales (eds.), The Psychosocial Development of Minority Group Children. New York: Brunner/Mazel, 1983.

Schofield, J. W., and Anderson, K. "Combining Quantitative and Qualitative Components of Research on Ethnic Identity and Intergroup Relations." In J. S. Phinney and M. J. Rotheram (eds.), Children's Ethnic Socialization: Pluralism and Development. Newbury Park, Calif.: Sage, 1989.

Skolnick, A., Baumrind, D., and Bronson, W. "Development in Sociocultural Contexts." Unpublished manuscript, University of California, Berkeley, 1990.

Stephan, C. W. "Mixed-Heritage Individuals: Ethnic Identity and Trait Characteristics." In M.P.P. Root (ed.), Racially Mixed People in America. Newbury Park, Calif.: Sage, 1992.

Sue, D., and Sue, S. "Cultural Factors in the Clinical Assessment of Asian Americans." Journal of Consulting and Clinical Psychology, 1987, 55, 479–487.

Weisner, T. S., Gallimore, R., and Jordan, C. "Unpackaging Cultural Effects on Classroom Learning: Native Hawaiian Peer Assistance and Child-Generated Activity." Anthropology and Education Quarterly, 1988, 19, 327–351.

White, W. G., and Chan, E. "A Comparison of Self-Concept Scores in Chinese and White Graduate Students and Professionals." Journal of Non-White Concerns in Personnel and Guidance, 1983, 11, 138–141.

Wong, R. "Family, Kinship, and Ethnic Identity of the Chinese in New York City, with Comparative Remarks on the Chinese in Lima, Peru and Manila, Philippines." Journal of Comparative Family Studies, 1985, 16, 231–254.

Yau, J., and Smetana, J. G. Chinese-American Adolescents' Reasoning About Cultural Conflicts." Journal of Adolescent Research, in press.

Youniss, J., and Smollar, J. Adolescents' Relations with Their Mothers, Fathers, and Friends. Chicago: University of Chicago Press, 1985.

Catherine R. Cooper is professor of psychology and education at the University of California, Santa Cruz.

Harley Baker is a graduate student in developmental psychology at the University of California, Santa Cruz.

Dina Polichar is a graduate student at the University of Washington.

Mara Welsh is a graduate student at the University of California, Riverside.

Research on father-adolescent relationships must move beyond demonstrations of links between father behavior and adolescent outcomes. The chapters in this volume raise issues that lead toward investigations of processes that may account for these links.

Father-Adolescent Relationships: From Phase 1 Findings to Phase 2 Questions

W. Andrew Collins

Interest in the distinctive and overlapping functions of fathers has been a promising thread running through family-oriented research for the past quarter century. The chapters in this volume give us some additional reasons for hopefulness and some specific suggestions that may bolster prospects for further progress in the future.

Before turning to those themes, though, let me offer as background some observations about where we have been in the study of fathers as distinctive and significant figures in adolescents' development. Several years ago, Collins and Russell (1991) reviewed the literature on parent-child relations in middle childhood and adolescence in hopes of discovering the critical dimensions of differentiation, if any, between adolescents' relationships with their mothers and with their fathers. They reached three conclusions that are especially relevant to the chapters in this volume.

The first was that virtually all of the research involving fathers had been built around one of two ideas: the *interchangeability* of mothers and fathers in caregiving and socialization or the *complementarity* of the distinctive contributions of each parent on key aspects of socialization. Interchangeability hypotheses were more common in studies of very young children because of an interest in caregiving alternatives. In middle childhood and adolescence, however, complementarity hypotheses were dominant because of their links to ideas about the emergence of social gender differences at puberty.

Second, in these studies there was evidence of some similarities and some differences in behaviors between mothers and fathers, and many of these were

NEW DIRECTIONS FOR CHILD DEVELOPMENT, no. 62, Winter 1993 © Jossey-Bass Publishers

consistent with the complementarity of socializing influences. There were also a number of instances in which socialization theorists had expected to find differences, but none emerged (for example, in parental encouragement of achievement). In noting these patterns, however, Collins and Russell recognized two distinct limitations to the available information: (1) few if any studies involved samples of sufficient size to address some of the most specific complementarity hypotheses—namely, the expectation of gender of parent and gender of child interactions; and (2) there was little diversity of samples to help scholars judge whether the distinctive characteristics of father-adolescent relations reflected a socialization principle or simply a cultural artifact.

Third, and most relevant, most of the findings were phase 1 findings: group differences or significant correlations involving indicators of father behavior and some condition or outcome referring to adolescent offspring. Much rarer were phase 2 findings, in which the pathway or processes linking father variables to adolescent variables are explicitly spelled out and examined. In particular, the implications of father behavior or attitudes for the nature and quality of dyadic or joint functioning with the adolescent were rarely examined as an intervening process for particular outcomes.

An example is the familiar contention that fathers are likely to behave more deferentially toward daughters at puberty stage in order to facilitate socialization to gender-appropriate behavior. Findings from studies of European American adolescents indicate increased distance from both parents as a function of a daughter's pubertal maturation, but some findings indicate that this distance takes different forms and persists longer in father-daughter than in mother-daughter relationships (for example, Hill, 1988; Steinberg, 1988). It is not known, however, whether the apparently greater persistence of changes in the father-daughter relationship implies a qualitatively different affective disruption in father-daughter interaction than occurs in mother-daughter interaction. Neither is it known how this distancing is perceived by either father or daughter or how it may be linked to their perceptions of what is appropriate and comfortable for each of them. These gaps are significant, because it is at the level of the day-to-day interdependencies constituting adolescents' relationships with mothers and fathers that some insights might be gained into the significance of relationships with fathers in adolescents' lives. To date, though, the linking processes and mechanisms—the phase 2 questions—have been raised more in the way of speculation than in terms of research findings or research designs.

This possibly idiosyncratic reading of the research to date offers some clues as to why these chapters are a sign of useful new directions in research on fathers and adolescents. Two themes stand out most in this regard: the need to attend to relationships and the need to do so in the context of cultural and historical scripts for the conduct of relationships.

Attending to Relationships

First, these studies give explicit attention to relationships, rather than only to individual outcomes, in considering the correlates of father behavior, and this could be a useful step toward addressing phase 2 questions more extensively. Larson (Chapter One) specifically sampled times when father and adolescent were together and considered them in conjunction with times spent alone, which they then linked back to father expectancies and, speculatively, forward to adolescent outcomes. Montemayor, McKenry, and Julian (Chapter Four) and Shulman and Klein (Chapter Three) asked for reports of relationships by father or offspring, respectively, and Shulman and Klein compared adolescents' perceptions of relationships with fathers to relationships with mothers. Almeida and Galambos (Chapter Two) found longitudinal decreases in the amount and kind of involvement between fathers and adolescents. Across cultural groups, Cooper and her co-workers (Chapter Five) found more informality and openness of communication with mothers, siblings, and friends than with fathers, all within the framework of fairly pronounced familistic values.

To be sure, this is still phase 1 information, with correlations between father variables and relationship variables substituted for father-adolescent outcome correlations. But each author has also offered ideas about possible phase 2 processes—pathways linking father behavior, through relationships, to particular outcomes. Larson proposed that fathers' behavior as recreation leader sets the expectation that "fun" is the key ingredient of time together. Warmth of relationship, then, moderates opportunities for father-adolescent interaction because of the incompatibility of fun and negative affect in less warm relationships. Thus the pathway from father behavior to adolescent outcome may go through warmth to opportunities for interaction and then to adolescent psychosocial outcome. Almeida and Galambos further note the possibility that variations in perceived acceptance across time may reflect variations not in warmth, but in other expectations of adolescents (such as independence or achievement) that also contribute to significant developmental outcomes.

A second possibility, suggested by Shulman and Klein, is that fathers' frequency, duration, and diversity of interactions with adolescents constitutes relatively lower involvement, compared with mothers. Because discussion of adolescents' own ideas and decisions constitutes a larger, more distinctive proportion of time with fathers than with mothers, the father may be perceived as differentially encouraging independence, thus facilitating individuation and identity striving. Here the pathway is through the complementarity of mothers' and fathers' relative emphasis on independence versus dependence. The suggestion by Almeida and Galambos that changing patterns of interaction may indicate altered functions of fathers during adolescence is consistent with this view.

Note that both of these possibilities derive from the well-established and often cited finding regarding fathers' more limited time with adolescents and emphasis on recreational rather than instrumental activities. But the pathways through relationships differ in that Larson emphasizes affective dimensions and Shulman emphasizes the topical content of interactions.

Finally, Montemayor, McKenry, and Julian offer alternative hypotheses linking fathers' developmental issues to adolescent outcomes. Here fathers' midlife crises could have one of two relational implications: (1) greater interest in and openness to adolescent offspring or (2) less attentiveness and responsiveness to adolescent developmental issues. The findings imply that the latter may be more likely, although more examination of other possibilities is needed, as the authors point out. One obvious possibility to be pursued is that adolescent developmental change contributes to fathers' midlife issues, a hypothesis that is consistent with findings from Silverberg and Steinberg (1990).

A relevant theme yet to be addressed is the relational system in which father-adolescent dyads are embedded. Mothers are more than a comparison point for father-adolescent relationships. What is the impact of each parent on the other's attitudes toward and involvement with adolescents, and what is the impact of each parent's explicit or implicit expectations regarding the adolescent's behavior and attitude toward the other parent? These second-order attitudinal effects have been well documented in the study of early relationships. As an example, Cohen (1981) has described a phenomenon called "father-gilding," in which mothers manage and interpret fathers' behavior to young children, especially when the father is frequently absent or absent for long periods. The mother may assure the child that father will be interested in what is happening with him or her and may prompt the father to ask specific questions about these activities. Second-order processes are likely to occur in different forms and via different and more complex pathways during adolescence, but they are almost certainly significant at these older ages as well. More attention should also be given to father-adolescent interaction when the two are together with the mother or other family members—a far more common occurrence than father-adolescent time alone.

These findings thus provide several leads for proceeding to phase 2 in the understanding of links between father behavior and adolescent development—links that draw attention to dyadic interactions as the locus of processes determining the cumulative outcomes of these interactions. It is important to note that many of the issues in the study of fathers and adolescents pertain equally to studies of other family relationships (such as mother-adolescent relationships). This buttresses Collins and Russell's (1991) argument that a better understanding is needed of the nature, significance, and interrelations of the multiple close relationships in which adolescents are implicated as a prerequisite to moving beyond phase 1 questions about the impact of families in development.

Contextualizing Relationships

The second theme emerging from these chapters is the contextualization of father-adolescent relationships. Traditional behavioral research is frequently criticized as being "decontextualized," but the referent for this term is not always as clear, as would be helpful. In the chapters in this volume, however, several specific aspects of the contexts in which fathers relate to adolescents have been examined. Montemayor and collaborators invoke fathers' own developmental issues as a factor in the quality and significance of relationships with adolescents. As with other work on parent factors in relationships during adolescence, this recognizes that relationships are composed of two individuals who follow distinct, as well as interrelated, developmental trajectories. Larson notes work roles and experiences as a context and specifically links them to an important mediating variable: fathers' expectations about time spent at home and with family, vis à vis typical experiences in the workplace. Cooper and her collaborators make the most frontal attack by looking to cultural contexts that subject father-adolescent interactions to constraints, demands, and opportunities that are sometimes distinct from those pertaining to other close relationships.

Behavioral scientists typically are novices at the kind of ecological analysis required to fully incorporate contextual variation into the understanding of the impact of father-adolescent relationships. Yet, clearly, the phase 2 questions—the business of why and how a particular contextual condition is linked to the impact of father-adolescent interactions—require attention to the pathways from context to outcome.

Anthropological and historical research (for example, Harkness and Super, in press; Parke and Stearns, 1993) reminds us what a laborious task this is and also provides good examples of why it is essential. To raise some possibilities, one starting place would be the recurring observation that a common (even predominant) activity for middle-class European American fathers and adolescents is playful, recreational activity. Some key questions are:

• When, historically, did play and recreation become the modal interaction pattern between fathers and adolescents (as opposed to the father's role as distant provider and disciplinarian)? What does this historical shift tell us about the meaning of this pattern? Larson has provided evidence that, in European American middle-class families, fathers and adolescents view these events somewhat differently. The ramifications of those different perceptions for the developmental significance of father-adolescent interactions are a priority for further research.

• Has this shift occurred to a similar extent across cultural groups, and, if not, what is the significance of the continuation of patterns more typical of these groups? The findings from Cooper and her collaborators suggest that the predominant activities are different in some non-European groups compared with European American groups.

• What implications should be expected for adolescent development? It has been argued, for example, that this apparent historical evolution in model interaction patterns from European American fathers has increased the ambiguity in the father's role and that, to some degree, this ambiguity carries a potential for self-indulgence and exploitiveness by fathers. Perhaps this tendency accounts for Larson's findings about the demand quality and perceived similarity to time with "buddies" in fathers' expectations about time with adolescents.

Other questions and emphases are possible. The preceding points are mentioned only to underscore the idea that, to get at the meaning of fathers' relationships with adolescents, one must understand how the circumstances of their lives create demands, opportunities, and constraints experienced by each with respect to the other.

The efforts of the past quarter century have yielded an accumulation of interesting and provocative findings that weave fathers explicitly into the fabric of information about families of adolescents. The themes raised by these chapters are reason for optimism that, in the next decade, the understanding of what those findings mean is likely to grow, both in social and cultural perspective and in terms of the aspects of father-adolescent relationships that have significant implications for the individual lives of both.

References

Cohen, G. "Culture and Educational Achievement." Harvard Educational Review, 1981, 51, 270–285.

Collins, W. A., and Russell, G. "Mother-Child and Father-Child Relationships in Middle Childhood and Adolescence: A Developmental Analysis." Developmental Review, 1991, 11, 1–38.

Harkness, S., and Super, C. M. "The Cultural Foundations of Fathers' Roles: Evidence from Kenya and the U.S." In B. S. Hewlett (ed.), The Father-Child Relationship: Anthropological Perspectives. Hawthorne, N.Y.: Aldine de Gruyter, in press.

Hill, J. P. "Adapting to Menarche: Familial Control and Conflict." In M. R. Gunnar and W. A. Collins (eds.), Development During the Transition to Adolescence: The Minnesota Symposia on Child Psychology. Vol. 21. Hillsdale, N.J.: Erlbaum, 1988.

Parke, R. D., and Stearns, P. N. "Fathers and Childrearing: A Historical Analysis." In J. Modell, G. Elder, Jr., and R. D. Parke (eds.), Child Development and History: An Interdisciplinary Dialogue. New York: Cambridge University Press, 1993.

Silverberg, S. B., and Steinberg, L. "Psychological Well-being of Parents with Early Adolescent Children." Developmental Psychology, 1990, 26, 658–666.

Steinberg, L. "Reciprocal Relation Between Parent-Child Distance and Pubertal Maturation." Developmental Psychology, 1988, 24, 122–128.

W. ANDREW COLLINS is professor in the Institute of Child Development, University of Minnesota.

INDEX

Adolescent-father interactions: vs. adolescent-mother interactions, 42–43; assumptions of developmental psychologists, 27; asymmetry of, 17; conflict in, 29, 33, 37; contextualizing, 95; continuity and change in, 27–38; cross-cultural comparison of, 73–90; differentiation, critical dimensions of, 91–92; enjoyment of, 15–17; enjoyment vs. warmth in, 17–19; and father's testosterone level, 65, 66, 67, 70; frequency and type of, 46–47; interpersonal perceptions of, 29–30, 33, 37; interrelationship with mother, 94; main issue in, 21; during midlife of father, 63–65; multidimensional approach to, 28; and parental authority, 30; play in, 53, 95–96; positive affect as a precondition for, 19; quality of, 29, 32–33; quantity of, 28–29, 32; relationships vs. individual outcomes in, 93. *See also* Adolescents; Fathers

Adolescents: communication with families and peers, in other cultures, 75–76, 79–84; daily lives of, 10–11; enjoyment of time with fathers, 15–17; familistic values of, in other cultures, 78–79; fathers' involvement with, 42; interactions with fathers and mothers, frequency and type, 46–47; in other cultures, 73–74; parents' respect and support for independence of, 48, 51; positive emotions about competence, 44; separateness in, 43; separation-individuation of, 41–55; time shared by fathers and, 13–14

Affect: positive, as a precondition for interaction, 19; measure of, 12, 14

Ainsworth, M. D. S., 52

Alessandri, S. M., 30, 37

Alienation, 7, 8, 20

Almeida, D. M., 29, 31, 32, 37

Anderson, K., 86

Archer, J., 66

Armentrout, J., 33

Arnold, K. D., 64, 67

Asmussen, L., 11, 21

Authority, parental, 30

Autonomy. *See* Independence, adolescent

Averill, J. R., 70

Azmitia, M., 75, 85, 86

Azuma, H., 85

Bales, J. R., 2

Bales, R. F., 42

Balswick, J. O., 67

Bardis, P. D., 75

Barnes, H. L., 67

Barnett, R. C., 64

Baumrind, D., 74

Becker, J. B., 66

Belsky, J., 41

Berkowitz, D., 44

Berman, P. W., 1

Bernard, J., 8

Bernstein, I. S., 70

Bird, G. A., 32

Bird, G. W., 32

Blass, R. B., 44, 53

Blatt, S. J., 44, 53

Blechman, E. A., 70

Blehar, M., 52

Block, J., 27, 36, 41

Block, J. H., 27, 36, 41

Blos, P., 43, 55

Blyth, D. A., 12

Borland, D. C., 60

Bosse, H., 4

Bowen, G. L., 63

Breadwinners, role of men as, 8, 42, 52; continuing influence of, 10; job as an end in itself, 8–9

Brim, O. G., 60, 61

Bronson, W., 74

Bronstein, P., 55

Brooks-Gunn, J., 17

Brownlee, J. R., 1, 28, 36, 41, 52

Buchanan, C. M., 66

Burger, G., 33

Burke, L., 54

Callan, V., 17

Chan, E., 75

Charnov, E. L., 1

Chavez, V., 76

Children's Report of Parental Behavior Inventory (CRPBI), 33

ORDERING INFORMATION

NEW DIRECTIONS FOR CHILD DEVELOPMENT is a series of paperback books that presents the latest research findings on all aspects of children's psychological development, including their cognitive, social, moral, and emotional growth. Books in the series are published quarterly in Fall, Winter, Spring, and Summer and are available for purchase by subscription and individually.

SUBSCRIPTIONS for 1993 cost $54.00 for individuals (a savings of more than 25 percent over single-copy prices) and $75.00 for institutions, agencies, and libraries. Please do not send institutional checks for personal subscriptions. Standing orders are accepted.

SINGLE COPIES cost $17.95 when payment accompanies order. (California, New Jersey, New York, and Washington, D.C., residents please include appropriate sales tax.) Billed orders will be charged postage and handling.

DISCOUNTS FOR QUANTITY ORDERS are available. Please write to the address below for information.

ALL ORDERS must include either the name of an individual or an official purchase order number. Please submit your order as follows:
   Subscriptions: specify series and year subscription is to begin
   Single copies: include individual title code (such as CD59)

MAIL ALL ORDERS TO:
   Jossey-Bass Publishers
   350 Sansome Street
   San Francisco, California 94104-1342

FOR SINGLE-COPY SALES OUTSIDE OF THE UNITED STATES, CONTACT:
   Maxwell Macmillan International Publishing Group
   866 Third Avenue
   New York, New York 10022-6221

FOR SUBSCRIPTION SALES OUTSIDE OF THE UNITED STATES, contact any international subscription agency or Jossey-Bass directly.

OTHER TITLES AVAILABLE IN THE
NEW DIRECTIONS FOR CHILD DEVELOPMENT SERIES
William Damon, Editor-in-Chief

Statement of Ownership, Management and Circulation

(Required by 39 U.S.C. 3685)

1A. Title of Publication: NEW DIRECTIONS FOR CHILD DEVELOPMENT

1B. PUBLICATION NO.: 0 1 9 5 2 2 6 9

2. Date of Filing: 12/13/93

3. Frequency of Issue: Quarterly

3A. No. of Issues Published Annually: Four (4)

3B. Annual Subscription Price: $54.00 (personal) $75.00 (institutional)

4. Complete Mailing Address of Known Office of Publication *(Street, City, County, State and ZIP+4 Code) (Not printers)*

350 Sansome Street, San Francisco, CA 94104-1342 (San Francisco County)

5. Complete Mailing Address of the Headquarters of General Business Offices of the Publisher *(Not printer)*

(above address)

6. Full Names and Complete Mailing Address of Publisher, Editor, and Managing Editor *(This item MUST NOT be blank)*

Publisher *(Name and Complete Mailing Address)*

Jossey-Bass Inc., Publishers (above address)

Editor *(Name and Complete Mailing Address)*

William Damon, Meikeljohn Hall, Brown University, 159 George Street, Providence, RI 02912

Managing Editor *(Name and Complete Mailing Address)*

Lynn D. Luckow, President, Jossey-Bass Inc., Publishers (address above)

7. Owner *(If owned by a corporation, its name and address must be stated and also immediately thereunder the names and addresses of stockholders owning or holding 1 percent or more of total amount of stock. If not owned by a corporation, the names and addresses of the individual owners must be given. If owned by a partnership or other unincorporated firm, its name and address, as well as that of each individual must be given. If the publication is published by a nonprofit organization, its name and address must be stated.) (Item must be completed.)*

Full Name	Complete Mailing Address
Macmillan, Inc.	55 Railroad Avenue Greenwich, CT 06830-6378

8. Known Bondholders, Mortgagees, and Other Security Holders Owning or Holding 1 Percent or More of Total Amount of Bonds, Mortgages or Other Securities *(If there are none, so state)*

Full Name	Complete Mailing Address
same as above	same as above

9. For Completion by Nonprofit Organizations Authorized To Mail at Special Rates *(DMM Section 424.12 only)*
The purpose, function, and nonprofit status of this organization and the exempt status for Federal income tax purposes *(Check one)*

☐ (1) Has Not Changed During Preceding 12 Months ☐ (2) Has Changed During Preceding 12 Months *(If changed, publisher must submit explanation of change with this statement.)*

10. Extent and Nature of Circulation *(See instructions on reverse side)*	Average No. Copies Each Issue During Preceding 12 Months	Actual No. Copies of Single Issue Published Nearest to Filing Date
A. Total No. Copies *(Net Press Run)*	1,326	1,358
B. Paid and/or Requested Circulation 1. Sales through dealers and carriers, street vendors and counter sales	250	139
2. Mail Subscription *(Paid and/or requested)*	466	485
C. Total Paid and/or Requested Circulation *(Sum of 10B1 and 10B2)*	716	624
D. Free Distribution by Mail, Carrier or Other Means Samples, Complimentary, and Other Free Copies	66	66
E. Total Distribution *(Sum of C and D)*	782	690
F. Copies Not Distributed 1. Office use, left over, unaccounted, spoiled after printing	544	668
2. Return from News Agents	0	0
G. TOTAL *(Sum of E, F1 and 2—should equal net press run shown in A)*	1,326	1,358

11. I certify that the statements made by me above are correct and complete

Signature and Title of Editor, Publisher, Business Manager, or Owner

Larry Ishii

Larry Ishii Vice President

PS Form 3526, January 1991   *See instructions on reverse*